Companies Can
Do Yoga Too

To my teachers and their teachers

Companies Can Do Yoga Too

By Marion Bevington

Build A Flexible Business That's Fit For The Future (Yoga Pants Optional!)

How to Implement Cultural Change to Grow in Business, Build Resilience, Lead Authentically and Increase Profits

ISBN-13: 978-1-537039-82-4

A Note to You, the Reader

Register For Updates

Welcome to this, my first published book. In the hope that you'll find it really useful, there's one thing that I highly recommend you do before you get started. Go to this special webpage designed just for you the reader, and register online for free updates, worksheets and activity sheets to add real value and find your other BONUS gifts to help you on your journey.

Calculate the hidden cost of sickness and ill health in your organisation with our free guide to the ROI.

Do you want to:

• Raise your Employee Job Satisfaction by 20%

• Improve your Employee Retention

• Sustain your Cultural Change

Complementary charts and worksheets are available to complete online or download to guide you through the book and keep you on track.

A free quiz to identify your dosha and design your own personalised yoga routine.

"Yoga at your desk"

Get your 15min personal routine to do right now.

10% off training, classes and workshops.

Register now and here we go – you're off!

Click to Register HERE for Exclusive Updates!

www.corporateyogalondon.com

Contents

Foreword

As a business coach I've spent the last 20 years helping people find their true calling in life.

My book Double Your Income Doing What You Love has become a best seller because of its advice on how to look within and find what makes your heart sing – and then find a way for you to monetize it. And I love nothing more than meeting people who believe this too, who have walked the walk, discovered their inner passion and now make their living that way.

So I'm particularly proud to write this foreword for *Companies Can Do Yoga Too!* The title is intriguing because it's indicating how companies can be healthy! You know that there are certain ways that your employees are unhealthy, represented by absenteeism and presenteeism... This IS COSTING you MONEY.

If you are a CEO, if you are a human resources specialist or manager, or if you are in charge of HR for any business, then you can use the calculator found at the website www.corporateyogalondon.com to determine EXACTLY how much money you can save by having a healthy company and by having a healthy workforce.

This is so powerful because it is like a big secret; it's an unknown LOSS.

This will NOT show up on your balance sheet because there is not an accounting entry for "sick work force" and so there is no way that you can see how much it is costing you and your business!

It doesn't matter how carefully you study your financial figures it doesn't matter how deeply you look into your financial reports it doesn't matter how carefully you look at your financial statements you will not see this anywhere!

But it is there and it is a hidden ugly cost which is damaging and hurting your company greatly.

Go to www.corporateyogalondon.com and use this calculator and find out exactly how much money you can save by using these techniques because then you will understand why you need to use Marion Bevington and Corporate Yoga London to help your company save this revenue, thrive in the current market and grow in to the great business you want to lead.

I am proud to say that my book – Double Your Income Doing What You Love – is on her desk. And I'm happy to reveal that one of the very first printed copies of Companies Can Do Yoga Too is on mine.

Raymond Aaron

NY Times Best Selling Author

Acknowledgements

This book has evolved over many years, during this time I have accumulated many debts to many people, only a few of which I have space to acknowledge here.

I dedicate this book for all of my family, friends and colleagues who have encouraged and supported me. I would like to offer my respect and sincere thanks for all of my yoga teachers and I want to give credit and recognition to: T.K.V. Desikachar, Mrs Armaiti Neriosang Desai, Dr. Jayadeva, Smt. Hansaji Yogendra, Dr. Robin Munro, Shri Deepak Gupta and Sarah Macintosh. I would like to acknowledge all of these teachers along side my students and support workers who served me during my Yoga teacher training and further studies at The Yoga Institute, Santacruz, Mumbai, and at the KYM Institute of Yoga Studies, Chennai, both schools are in India, also at The Yoga Biomedical Trust and Yoga Therapy Centre in London, here in the U.K.

I would like to specially mention some of my key mentors and friends including Andrea, Cheryl, Crystal, Máire, Margot, Miles and Sammy who have all been coaches and supporters of my most recent journey and my editor Richard White - I am indebted to all of you. My closest family and friends including my Mum, Terence, Glenn, David, Alan, Tsveta, Annie, Chris, Tracey, Simon and Carlos Duval! For simply being there for me and for your patience and love.

Finally to Raymond Aaron who has helped throughout the process of writing. Thanks for your guidance and encouragement. Writing of this book has been a collaborative exercise. Apart from the names mentioned, there are many others who contributed. I could not give all the names for want of time and space. I appreciate their help and thank them for their support.

Prologue

I met Marion in London in 2011 at a personal growth event. She's one of those perceptive people that seem to have a sixth sense about life. Straight talking but warm, someone you want on your team with a finely tuned ability to see things others couldn't. She'd give you a hug hello and immediately know you had a pain in your foot. She'd talk to you for a minute and seem to sense your inner mood.

When I found out she was a yoga teacher that made complete sense: in touch with the body and mind; feeling forces that others might miss.

However I wasn't expecting her to reveal that she'd had a former life as a geek. A pinstriped geek with just over twenty years working in IT in the City of London. Until this fully paid-up member of the rat race realised she was in the wrong job.

So she escaped to follow her passion in life – yoga. She got on a plane to India to study with Vedic gurus how to still the physical body to hear the subconscious mind, and rebalance her life after years in a high-powered low-fulfilment job.

Critically she realised that her former colleagues – all those other rats still trapped – needed to hear this message too. So she returned to The City as a yoga therapist and teacher to pass it on.

She realised that a book was the quickest way to help people, and we met when she enrolled into a public speaking coaching programme and she asked for my help with this book, as a copywriting expert. Now it is my privilege to introduce you to what I consider one of the more relevant books on business success you are likely to encounter.

So why should companies try yoga? When I met her I asked Marion if this was about using yoga to fix a crook neck and reduce sickness and absenteeism. Yes, she said. But there's more.

If you do it right, she said, it could also improve relationships, communication and innovation, create stronger teams, give managers the sort of authenticity that money just can't buy, and create an organisation that transforms into a 21st century powerhouse.

It's a set of simple disciplines that help centre the body and mind and make you fit on all levels to do business with a heightened sense of instinct and intuition. If ever there was a golden key to inspirational leadership, it comes from yoga and the principles it teaches.

So in this book she shows you how to explore your current set of beliefs about life and business. Then to challenge them, find your true values and guide your life in an authentic way that's true to yourself and to those around you.

Your mind is a powerful tool. Your beliefs and thoughts bring about a cascade of very real chemical and physical changes in your brain and the body. Marion shows you how you and others in your company can use simple yoga tools, theories and philosophies to create the optimum mind and body for business success.

She takes you right back to ancient Vedic wisdom with a simple system that explains how the body works on five different levels - the physical, the energetic body, the mental body, the intellectual body and finally the bliss body. These five levels influence human behaviour in all manner of ways, and yoga helps you manage all of them better.

She teaches you how to apply this wisdom in modern business settings, drawing upon her own experiences in the City of London as first a business woman and then a yoga teacher and therapist.

This is a complete and holistic approach to improving performance, productivity and growth both within the person and within the organisation. In every body, and in everybody.

In this digital age, it's more important than ever to have a clear and focused mind and heart-led collaborations. It's the only way, Marion contends, that you respect basic human needs and avoid information overload, confusion and uncertainty.

Having this still centre of calm amidst all the frenetic activity of 21st century business is the path to huge power and success.

Her methods will help you say goodbye to bad sleeping habits, poor diet and high stress and instead give you power and performance where you start your day wanting to get to work, energized and relaxed, and you go to bed with a profound sense of peace and achievement.

Whether you are a leader in an established business or a budding entrepreneur, this book will inspire you to take a positive approach to growing your productive profitable business and evolving as a human being.

And congratulations because you've discovered this book at exactly the right time to solve a problem that faces every trading business. Technology is moving at such a fast pace that humanity is having trouble keeping up. Men and women in boardrooms and management teams are having to deal with new ways of working, of dealing with customers and nurturing teams.

Those with dinosaur attitudes will fail. What's needed is enlightened thinking in business about 21st century relationships, engagement, authenticity and what it looks like to do the right thing.

Read this and you'll build a more resilient you. Apply it throughout your department and company and you'll have a stronger workforce with lower absenteeism and higher motivation. The end result will be a dynamic profitable business that has the edge on your competition because it's running on enlightenment.

I love Marion's enthusiasm for her subject. I love that she wants to help the corporate world develop its consciousness. She wants to save the suits. And I am behind her 100%.

Andrea Sangster,

Copywriting Shenanigans Expert

Copy Made Simple

Introduction

"Greatness is not this wonderful, esoteric, illusive, God-like feature that only the special among us will ever taste. You know, it's something that truly exists in all of us. It's very simple."

- Will Smith

Companies really can do Yoga too, now obviously I'm not referring to the "putting your leg behind your ear" style of Yoga, that so swiftly comes to people's minds when I mention this book title to them. Yoga is practical in so many other ways, not just for the physical body. What about the mind? Right now with the digital revolution at full speed and still accelerating, we are all in real danger of information overload. In any overloaded system it's impossible to identify the crucial components or ingredient needed to fulfil the purpose, the purpose of the work, of the system, of your life!

Yoga is about experience, looking at how your experience effects and affects your work and life, focusing on what it is and not what it *should* be. It is about enriching your experience of your life-experience!

What is yoga? The root is shared with our English word "yoke". To yoke means to bind together and the desired outcome can then be achieved even if it was previously unobtainable...

The ploughing of a field is impossible for one man, difficult for one ox, hard work for two oxen and one man – but when the oxen are yoked together it is possible and easy. Yoga is all about connection, about our thoughts, our words and actions, how they connect us to objects, to ideas, to others, to the world and how that connection impacts our experience, affects our life.

Yoga – To Yoke Together

It is such a delight to be able to write about yoga and how to apply its wisdom to the whole of an organisation for the mutual growth and contribution of all involved. This is a practical book, explaining how to apply yogic wisdom to both business and to everyday life experiences. Contemporary psychological and neurological theory, studies and findings are consistently upholding the efficacy of the science and

14

art of yoga as a powerful tool for development, growth and evolution. But that's not the whole story; yoga is first and foremost about action. It gives you choices in your mind and in your body, and so frees you up to explore the spirit in which you live, work, rest and play.

Good people make good business and better people make better businesses, how can a business help its people become better?

"It feels good. Kinda like when you have to shut your computer down, just sometimes when it goes crazy, you just shut it down and when you turn it on, it's OK again.

- Ellen DeGeneres

If you are curious about life, if you are fascinated with people, then having access to yoga which is in fact the subjective experience of thousands of people over thousands of years will not disappoint you.

How do we do what we do?

How do we think?

How do we learn?

And how do outstanding people in any field get consistently brilliant results?

To answer these and other questions let's explore (a fraction of) what yoga has to offer. The goal is excellence, expansion and evolution for all.

Yoga, as we know it today, can be dated back to over 5000 years ago. It draws upon the insights and wisdom passed down from many ancient sages, there is one such sage called Patanjali. Patanjali is believed to have compiled his Yoga Sutra around the 3rd or 4th century BC. Archaeological evidence and the study of ancient scriptures suggest that yoga was practiced in ancient India as early as 3000 BC.

Patanjali wrote The Yoga Sutra, which is by far the most definitive text on the philosophy of classical yoga, and yet very little is known about Patanjali. In fact, the identity of this sage and scholar is still being debated in academic circles.

Yoga has given rise to a whole host of tools and techniques that can be used both personally and professionally. It is now recognised internationally and in many fields, such as fitness and sport, health and wellbeing, business and education, as a brilliant way to enable us not only to reach out and influence others, but much more powerfully to reach within to unify and empower the different parts of ourselves.

You now have access to many of these tools and techniques, in this book and many more on the website. I am sharing with you the theory, concepts and processes, so you can take the ideas and make them your own in the way that suits you best. Don't just take my word for it – yoga is all about experience – your experience not mine! I would be doing a dis-service if I didn't remind you that the power of this amazing experiential science is in the experiencing. It is drawn from the experience of many. It is not a doctrine, not authoritative instruction, not just a set of rules and regulation, not because it's how it's done in traditional or cultural narratives, none of these are truth. Your experience is your truth, so don't just listen to me – well read me. Think about what you read and then how it relates to you and your experiences in life and of life.

Your body and mind seem constant, but are changing all the time, like a river – incessant, ceaseless activity, moment-by-moment change. Yet you have a fundamental awareness of this, and that awareness is something at a very deep level that is always the same. Thoughts and physiology are intimately connected (mind and body), so your thinking affects your physiology, your physical and mental health, your wellbeing, and they all in turn affect your thoughts.

A belief, simply stated, is a repeated thought, that's all it is and yet what you believe deeply affects what you think, how you feel and how you act. All of this is brings your experience of life.

What are the consequences of your beliefs?

What actions flow from them?

Are they useful and do they serve you?

Faith in what you believe and knowing (through experience) that it serves you is your truth. When your truth is based on your own experience, only then is it of real value to you.

In this ever-changing world, with more technologies than ever, with more channels of communication than ever with more information than ever before, the challenge of operating and leading a successful and growing business is huge. This book is your guide to exploring and finding ways to succeed and grow; in yourself and in business today.

A resilient workforce, authentic leadership, conscious and transparent values and purposes are just some of the gifts you and your company can achieve through the thoughtful and mindful application of even a few of the powerful and wise ideas brought to you from this yogic treasure trove of possibilities.

I have aimed here to bring a sample of the core yogic concepts compiled by Patanjali and some practical uses. I hope that you too will uncover some precious wisdom that serves you in your own development and evolution as well as that of your company.

For a more comprehensive map of yoga, you can find an additional resources section on the website which includes suggestions on books, courses, training, workshops and, videos.

Subscribe to the website to register for your free updates, reports, personalised yoga routines, guided meditations and so much more, at
http://www.corporateyogalondon.com/exclusiveupdates

And now, using the very first of Patanjalis yoga sutras, which when translated means - Now, after having done prior preparation through life and other practices, the study and practice of Yoga begins.

"Atha Yoga Anusharsanam"

Chapter 1

The Modern Business

*"If you want to change the fruits,
you will first have to change the roots.
If you want to change the visible, you must first
change the invisible."*

- T. Harv Eker

Modern businesses today are focused on growth, not at any cost but at less cost.

A successful business is one that has growing profits year on year. Achieving this means simultaneous growth in top-line revenue and bottom-line profitability. Above and beyond this is the need for expansion and innovative growth into the ever changing technological evolution we are experiencing.

A Revolution From Toxteth to Timbuktu

And in the real world, on nearly every corner of the world, from London to L.A., from Amazonia to Zanzibar, from Toxteth to Timbuktu, there is nowhere that you can go without seeing someone talking, texting or surfing the Internet on their Smartphone, laptop or tablet. Information Technology (IT) has become ubiquitous, and is changing every aspect of how we live.

Recent advances in our ability to communicate and process information in digital form – a series of developments we can describe as the "IT revolution" – are reshaping the economies, businesses and societies of almost every country, every nook and cranny of the world.

There are many organisations that have achieved impressive levels of innovation and workforce efficiency in recent years, however they still require more. To stay competitive and continue to grow, CEOs and leadership teams must strive to find breakthrough, leading edge performance and productivity gains from employees in this rapidly changing landscape powered by the IT revolution.

The Amazing Shrinking World

Globalisation compounds the accelerating changes in technology. Every day we see the appearance of more innovative technologies; the opening up of new markets, and the pace of change is breath-taking. There is a feeling of always playing catch up, trying to purchase or update new devices, new apps; get more up-to-date training in the latest leadership trends and methodologies. Within companies, all companies, there is a need for new skills enabling businesses to harness, use and manage this change, and as if that wasn't enough, there is the added need for managing the stress that inherently grows alongside all of this.

Technology is now well and truly at the forefront of the modern world, creating new jobs and innovations, and there is social media and the multitude of networking sites; all of this allows more and more of us as individuals and companies to connect globally, not only to more people but also to access more information.

From Semi's To Smartphones

A timeline of the rapid transformation of how technological acceleration shows the exponential growth in change and in our reliance on these technologies in over two decades prior to 2017:

- 21 years ago: Internet commercialised
- 20 years ago: Mobile phones use the Internet
- 18 years ago: Google named the search engine of choice by PC magazine
- 15 years ago: Blackberry launched
- 12 years ago: Facebook launched
- 11 years ago: 100 million Wi-Fi chipsets sold
- 10 years ago: Twitter launched
- 9 years ago: iPhone introduced
- 7 years ago smart TV's appeared
- 6 years ago: 17 million smart tablets sold — estimated 100+ million by 2014
- Every 60 seconds: new apps tailored to users' specific needs created

Advances in Information Technology, or "the IT revolution", are driving an extraordinarily rapid decline in the cost and an exponential increase in the processing power of digital technologies.

The microprocessor, the brain behind the scenes, in my working life corporate digital processing and storage has gone from the size of a four-bed semi to a smartphone, and at the same time the speed and power have increased! Over the past two decades, the processing power of microprocessors has doubled roughly every six months.

From Dinosaur to Digital

The industrial age is as far away as the dinosaur age! Today's wireless digital age is here, has been for a while (recently rebranded from the information age) and is not going away anytime soon! Are you keeping up? Or is it keeping you up? Are your stress levels rising in line with technology levels?

To achieve the continuing growth in productivity and revenues, the top and bottom lines, organisations need to thrive and not just survive. Survival is a very stressful place to be; it's like being on the edge – thriving is well away from the edge, it's more relaxed, allows for grace, time for fun and enjoyment. When we thrive we have space time and energy for growth, for healing, for transformation, for "Re-Creation", so understanding the difference between thrive and survive helps to show us where the growth potential is – thriving and not in the protective stressful state that is surviving.

In order to thrive and grow you must understand the dramatic shifts underway in the work environment, which will allow you to refocus on enabling higher levels of workforce performance, and this means effectively managing that seemingly inherent stress and retaining or sometimes recovering the ability to flourish.

Change *Is* The New Normal

Today's work environment is in constant flux, meaning change is the new normal. For employees, that means changes in target markets, products, suppliers,

22

relationships, business objectives, organisation structure, work location, work teams, job role or manager alignments. Partly as a response to a more fluid and shifting business environment and a result of ubiquitous information and rapid technological advances, the predominant work of employees has become much more collaborative and at the same time knowledge-based.

While some firms may be tempted to hire an all-new workforce that is better able to perform in a collaborative, knowledge-based work environment, the needs of the workforce in place today are much more immediate. For businesses to maintain the foundation and current workloads is imperative. To grow you must at the same time acquire the new skills required to stay alive in the transformed workplace environment that's all around us. Improving – or simply maintaining – workforce productivity means you need to accept and take advantage of the fact that the work environment has changed, and your underlying approaches to employee development, work roles, management, leadership and technology must also change.

Stress is all the RAGE!

Improving executive, leadership, workforce performance and productivity is a central focus of this book. Psychological, neurological and physiological – in fact *multilogical* studies show that the mind and body are intrinsically linked. We really don't need any scientists to tell us that the impact of stress has become more and more prevalent, as the growth in diseases and health conditions that result from this same stress seems to match the rapid change we see in the way we work and live.

> *"It is health that is real wealth and not pieces of gold and silver."*
>
> - Mahatma Gandhi

Positive Outlook Brings Real Wealth

As mental health declines, physical health can also worsen, and vice versa. A positive outlook and healthier living can maintain a state of good health in both mind and body. Through our day-to-day experiences we can continue to refine our understanding of the changing work environment, evolving skills, adapting requirements, and continuously identifying how to manage the challenges of change are essential to improving company-wide performance and productivity.

Charles Atlas, described as "The world's most perfectly developed man" said this so eloquently...

> *"You are what you are because of your past daily habits. Day by day you must make or break your body. You either build it up or tear it down. If your objective is to build up your HEALTH, STRENGTH and PERSONAL POWER, you must now conserve your energy for the acquisition of new and better health habits. Once they become fixed, you will experience no difficulty in retaining HEALTH and STRENGTH all through life.*

24

To overcome your past injurious habits and develop better ones, you must bring your entire ATTENTION to the matter; you must think intently of the motives and the outcome involved and thus occupy your mind with better things, turning away from past habits toward freedom. REMEMBER, ALL EVIL HABITS MAY BE DESTROYED BY THE PERSON WHO REALLY DESIRES TO CONQUER THEM."

- Charles Atlas

Real Health Is Resilience

Identifying and combining best practices for personal and professional resilience through self-development from ancient and modern science of all types, all ologies, will equip senior leaders, executives, managers and their teams with insight and solutions they can act on, transforming all areas and all levels in every type of organisation.

Ancient Wisdom - How it Can Help You

Yoga is an ancient system and philosophy that everyone can practice, regardless of age, gender or ability. It originated in India over five thousand years ago, and in our hectic and often chaotic modern world many people are still today taking "time out" to practice it. It offers a systematic and entirely holistic approach to body, mind and spirit, which can provide us with the tools to cope with any and all of the challenges life throws at us.

The Sanskrit word "*yoga*" is translated as "union". The practice of yoga helps to co-ordinate the breath, mind and body to encourage balance, both internally and externally. It promotes feelings of relaxation and ease. Another beautiful translation of the word yoga is "to attain what was previously unobtainable".

You do not have to be flexible to start practicing yoga. And my wish is to show you how you can use yoga and the wisdom within it to benefit without tying yourself, your body or your mind into knots!

In the West, the most widely taught form of yoga is *Hatha* Yoga. The physical practices that you find in most yoga classes offer students postures and movements to stretch, to strengthen and to flex the body, also encouraging the development of breathing ability and of the awareness of the breath, to relax and energise. The purpose of *Hatha* Yoga is a preparation for *Raja* Yoga to prepare the body and make it comfortable to facilitate meditation, which results in a calm, balanced and cleansed mind.

There are classically four forms of yoga: *Raja Yoga - which includes* (meditation), *Karma* Yoga (action), *Jnana Yoga* (knowledge) and *Bhakti* Yoga (devotion).

I have included a glossary toward the end of the book to help you in understanding any Sanskrit words I use in the main text. The glossary gives only the briefest description of the words but offers a more simple way as a means of introducing the concepts and supporting your understanding, as your read on you'll find more details, more colour added to the meaning of the words and hopefully more clarity.

By incorporating yoga techniques into your daily routine, you inevitably become aware of changes, some will be subtle and others not so subtle, but there will be changes in your approach to life, to how you feel, how you perceive the world around you and yourself in it and how you move and look. You may also begin to get a glimpse of a state of inner peace . . . your authentic self, your own true nature.

You may be drawn to yoga simply for health and fitness, or be seeking relief for a specific physical condition. You might want help with managing stress and improving mental strength, creativity and performance, or maybe you would like pregnancy yoga classes or exercises suitable for the less able-bodied. Whatever your objectives, there are yoga tools and techniques that can meet them.

"If you can breathe then you can do yoga"

- Krishnamacharya

Providing business-focused yoga training helps to get everyone engaged in achieving the business goals, by developing the skills and abilities to unify values and attitudes, and align and expand perspectives across the whole organisation. Yoga is an art and a science, providing the philosophy and theory, the tools and methods to support the aims and objectives of your company. The art is the application of the knowledge that efficiently and effectively achieves the desired goal.

The practice of meditation and the other yogic practices discussed in this book all help to develop mindfulness that will in turn enrich your leadership style. Mindfulness can improve leadership, especially in times of instability. An authentic and mindful leader can respond to change with focus and clarity, and avoid repeating costly mistakes.

The best leaders are authentic; they are transparent with their intentions, filled with integrity and have a seamless link between their adopted values, actions and behaviours.

Having a yogic perspective allows the whole 'company' to be understood as a single unit called the Business, and its components are the individuals that contribute to the expression of the whole, including executives, leaders, managers and workers. Also its clients and suppliers, in fact everyone involved, anyone who plays any role – regardless of how small or seemingly insignificant.

The intelligent and holistic approach of Corporate Yoga enables executives and leaders to not only harness perspectives from the top-line to the bottom-line, but also to tap into breakthrough performance and innovation without costly consulting or reinvention of the whole business.

I love this following poem by Rudyard Kipling and remember the first time I read it I was bothered by the final line – what about women and girls?! But I'll leave it as it is so the poetic timing and phrasing are not disrupted; I, too, will remain centred and not disturbed by it.

IF by Rudyard Kipling

IF you can keep your head when all about you
Are losing theirs and blaming it on you,
If you can trust yourself when all men doubt you,
But make allowance for their doubting too;
If you can wait and not be tired by waiting,
Or being lied about, don't deal in lies,
Or being hated, don't give way to hating,
And yet don't look too good, nor talk too wise:
If you can dream - and not make dreams your master;
If you can think - and not make thoughts your aim;
If you can meet with Triumph and Disaster
And treat those two impostors just the same;
If you can bear to hear the truth you've spoken
Twisted by knaves to make a trap for fools,
Or watch the things you gave your life to, broken,
And stoop and build 'em up with worn-out tools:

If you can make one heap of all your winnings
And risk it on one turn of pitch-and-toss,
And lose, and start again at your beginnings
And never breathe a word about your loss;
If you can force your heart and nerve and sinew
To serve your turn long after they are gone,
And so hold on when there is nothing in you
Except the Will which says to them: 'Hold on!'

If you can talk with crowds and keep your virtue,
' Or walk with Kings - nor lose the common touch,
if neither foes nor loving friends can hurt you,
If all men count with you, but none too much;
If you can fill the unforgiving minute
With sixty seconds' worth of distance run,
Yours is the Earth and everything that's in it,
And - which is more - you'll be a Man, my son!

Chapter 2

The Big Problems

When you look at the larger perspective of business in general, from the position we are all in today, then it is possible to observe general trends that impact everybody and every business.

Building the next generation of employees requires focusing on a new set of skills. In 2013 the CEB (a publicly traded company providing advisory services to businesses worldwide) analysed the key drivers of performance for more than 23,000 managers and employees across more than 40 organisations globally and found the ten core employee competencies that differentiate those best able to perform in the new work environment. The following graph gives a great indication of those key competencies identified and a clear picture of the focus needed when developing the workforce required to build a winning business of the future.

"Statistics suggest that when customers complain, business owners and managers ought to get excited about it. The complaining customer represents a huge opportunity for more business."

- Zig Ziglar

Top three trends of today's workplace:

1. Frequent Change
2. Interdependence
3. Knowledge working

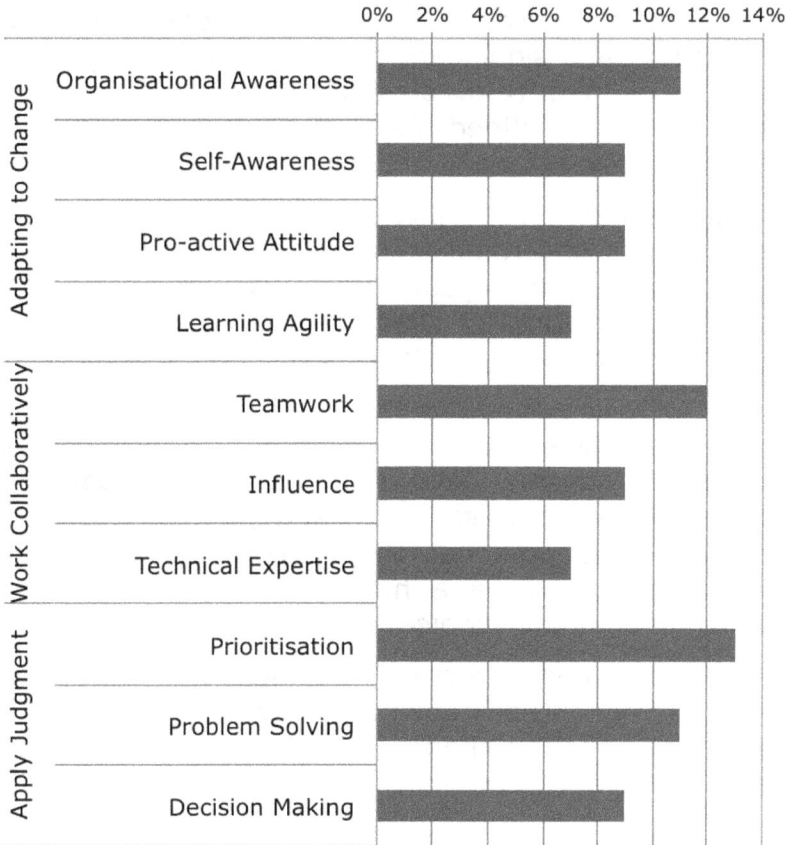

**Top 10 Competencies Driving
Empolyee Performance**

TREND 1: Frequent Change

Change is constant; it comes in many forms and is everywhere:

- Organisational downsizing and change
- Economic fluctuations
- Greater financial uncertainty

A persistent and common aspect of today's workplace is frequent and significant organisational change, both broadly defined (e.g. strategic objectives, markets) and narrowly defined (e.g. work teams, reporting relationships).

Economic uncertainty, regulatory shifting and adjustments and rapid technological changes all have consequences on your business objectives and strategies, leading to real changes in organisational structures, reporting relationships, work teams and processes.

In any high-change environment, established work processes become less relevant and valuable as objectives. As organisations change, adopting dynamic and flexible approaches that will pervade the entire organisation may be a huge challenge, but do you really have another choice?

Process and structure changes can disrupt, or even totally break down, long-standing employee networks. A high-change environment can reduce overall employee performance.

Change and ambiguity will derail productivity unless the leadership and management help employees to better anticipate, contextualise, prioritise and as a result, respond appropriately.

Human motivation is driven by basic human needs. Chapter 6 details what those needs are. One of the most basic needs is certainty (also known as security), so uncertainty and change can easily cause fear of change and de-motivation.

"You have to go deeper than belief to find faith"

- Eckhart Tolle

Letting Go Of Fear

At this point I think it's important to be clear on the difference between belief and faith. Initially they sound like similar concepts but when we put some context to them we can see the difference.

Many years ago the great Zumbrati had just completed a tightrope walk over the Niagara Falls. The conditions were bad, with high winds and driving rain, 'The Great Zumbrati' was greeted by an enthusiastic supporter, who urged him to make a return trip, this time pushing a wheelbarrow, which the spectator had thoughtfully brought along.

The Great Zumbrati was reluctant, and who wouldn't be given the terrible conditions? But the supporter pressed him, "You can do it – I know you can," he urged.

"You really believe I can do it?" asked Zumbrati.

"Yes – definitely – you can do it," the supporter gushed.

"Okay," said Zumbrati, "Get in the wheelbarrow ...."

It's possible that you've heard a supervisor or manager say, "You can do it" or "Make it happen". Maybe you yourself have said it? These words are very easy to say but the trust, belief and commitment that it can be done are much more difficult to earn.

Would you get in the wheelbarrow?

Belief - He is the Great Zumbrati, prepared, he looks confident and has making good progress so you believe he will make it across the rope for the second time. Belief is of the mind

Faith – This means getting into the wheelbarrow. Faith is of the heart.

Would your workforce willingly and confidently get into your wheelbarrow?

Here we meet a fundamental yogic concept, *Shraddha,* translated as Faith. More specifically this is faith cultivated through experience, knowledge and practice. This is not the same as blind faith; which is handed down by authority and adhered to because of fear.

Fear

In the media today we see constant images and messages that build a strong field of fear that we all have to live in – even if you don't watch television you still live in a community with those who do, so they have a strong field of fear that envelops you and your energies, and part of what this field does is maintain the belief, the fear that your life depends only upon external factors like the credit crunch, followed swiftly by the recession, then there is the bleak economic climate, terrorism, terrorism and more terrorism, bird flu, swine flu, computer viruses, even HIV/AIDS... the list is endless. What these all have in common is that they are influences that lie outside of yourself.

Make 'em change

It is a very common belief in our society that if you can just change your world from the outside, it will settle the unquiet and all of the disturbances on the inside. The problem with that thinking is that it imprisons you inside a notion that salvation is an outside job. So the need for certainty, which is a valuable basic human need when in balance with the real world, makes you cling ever more tightly to your identity, your achievements and your story, your history, which only end up separating you from what is really going to restore a sense of peace, reconnection and happiness.

"Striving in the outer removes us from flow."

- Ram Dass

To avoid that sense of fear caused by living in an unsafe world, and the sense of disappointment that can follow a great accomplishment, you must cultivate a relationship with who you are. Your identity that runs deeper than any attachments to your CV or your LinkedIn profile, deeper still than who you know, all of your Facebook friends, all of your Twitter followers, YouTube subscribers or who you have been (your email contacts list).

Shifting perspectives from outer to inner

True peace and balance come with an increasing awareness and awakening to who you are beyond all of your attachments, and to surrendering to the true you, your authentic self. This comes when you let go of the anxiety, let it wash through you and rejoin the flow of being in the moment. Happiness is not about a mechanism to "get there", but the discovery of who you are and where you are in the now; happiness comes from surrendering and embracing what is, without the immediate need to change it. I know this sounds so out of tune with how our society operates and how we are trained, but that's no reason to discard it. Society may believe this, but do you? Do you have faith in this way of operating?

We are all looking for relief from our racing mind, with all its fears, self-doubts and mistrust, mostly of who we really are beneath our striving and clinging to false ideas; of who and how we must be to be loved, to be free, to have our basic human needs, especially that certainty need, met by truth, and not just by the opinion of the majority.

Do you know any business owners, department heads or entrepreneurs whose business or big projects have failed? Maybe it's you? If so you'll know how they take this on as if they themselves have failed, regardless of the quality of leadership or management they exercised; then there are the parents or families who have a child who suffers in some way, they take on the suffering as if they have failed, regardless of how well they parented; then the unemployed husband who insists that there are no jobs out there, while his partner carries the whole load on her own back, feeling overwhelmed by the hopelessness that invades the atmosphere at home; then the grown son and daughter who are stressed over feelings of powerlessness in dealing with their parents' aging and decline. These are all very real examples of how your mind can get off track, leaving you winded in the aftermath of arriving at what had previously promised the certainty of happiness, all those happy ever afters, only to be knocked sideways by the unexpected.

"If you are deliberately trying to create a future that feels safe, you will willfully ignore the future that is likely."

- Seth Godin

The antidote: A mind in tune and in balance with the reality of the universe and of natural law.

Every now and then come moments of relief. Moments when you are transported from this prison cell, free again to roam the landscape of simply being in the flow of the present moment. In these brief moments were you are truly alive, awakened to a sense of belonging – belonging to the universe where all is well.

When was the last time you felt in flow? In touch with and an integral part of nature and her universe?

Maybe yours is so simple you can't recall it right now – it's such a natural place for us to be we so often hardly even notice it, or we give it no importance. One of mine was on a beach in India, I can picture it now, splashing around in the shallow waves, with the local kids, who can't swim but love to play in the shallow water, it makes me so happy. Just hanging out, with no place to 'get to.' We were just there with each other, playing, laughing, teasing, being kids. I remember the simplicity of it. There were no goals. There was just this kind of natural trust in the world, where everything was already all right. Having faith, that kind of faith – getting into your own wheelbarrow, not in some outside agency, in some other external concept – is not a blind faith in some organisation, institution or teacher. It is an inner feeling of certainty that you are moving in the right direction. You may not know exactly how your journey is unfolding, but have an inner intuition of walking steadily towards the goal of life. The "faith" of yoga is not one of "blind faith" as is the case of religions.

Experiential: In the Yoga Sutras you are instructed to not merely "believe" in anything. But you must test the ideas in your own inner laboratory, so that the "faith" of yoga is solely based on subjective and direct experience.

"If you create an act, you create a habit. If you create a habit, you create a character. If you create a character, you create a destiny."

- Andre Maurois

If you have ever practiced breath awareness and diaphragmatic breathing, did you find that it leads to a calm, quiet mind? That direct experience is the foundation of the "faith" in *Shraddha* – certain knowledge that continuing such breathing will, in the future, lead to a similar experience of calm and quiet.

Shraddha is a faith that you are moving in the right direction – unconditional trust that everything is as it is supposed to be right now, getting into that wheelbarrow and it is the only way to overcome the fear of change.

Once here, we can embrace all of life with its constant changes and we embrace it because we are aware that the universe and all of nature have got our back!

Beginning the journey to the place where we have that faith that "the universe has got my back!"

Yoga, A Guide To A Fulfilled Life

Vyasa was a great sage who wrote an amazing commentary on The Yoga Sutras (see chapter 3 for more information on The Sutras), many times longer than the original rich and terse text of Patanjali. Vyasa defined five states of *citta* (mind):

1) Restless (*ksipta*)

2) Listless (*mudha*)

3) Distracted (*viksipta*)

4) Focused (*ekagra*)

5) Controlled (*niruddha*)

The purpose of classifying the mind into five states is explained in depth in chapter 5. A model presented here will help you to understand the mind by identifying its varied states and activities.

The five states are a description of mind according to its development and refinement. This same model can also be used to describe a company's preparedness for inspired innovative practice and evolution.

This classification may well be helpful for managers and business owners who need to assess their company, the workforce and any individual employees' readiness for change and growth, so that you can find the appropriate tools, techniques and practices to ensure expansion and evolution of your company. It can also be helpful for all of us as individuals, especially those who desire or need to measure their own progress.

What enables us to spend more of our lives in the more desirable states of mind is the holistic practice of yoga, as defined by Patanjalis' eight steps, *Astanga*, including ethical conduct, asana, pranayama, and meditation. This will be discussed further in chapter 5.

Following the concepts and constructs with the teaching of Yoga will transport you to a fulfilled life, one in which you can begin to celebrate who you are – not fight with who you are not. So letting go of who you are not can be understood if you look more deeply at the concept of *Vairagya,* which means surrender, and the concept of *Vivekah,* meaning discrimination. With these two brilliant concepts you can begin to find what you need to let go of and how to do it.

Vairagya

Let go (Surrender to true reality). In order to let go of or even embrace the need for certainty and finding *Shraddha* in a constantly changing world, you can begin by examining your mind and recognise these stages in yourself. Can you choose your idea of what you have faith in? Of what you cling to of your own will? Or do the ideas that the external world throws at you disturb you too much to remain focused on your own ideas and clear about your goals?

Vivekah

Discrimination. If you can choose your idea and stay with it, hold it in mind, concentrating without being disturbed, then it's a short step from there to complete control, which can inhibit all movements of the mind. When you reach that stage, and continue to practice, then it is only natural to pass into *Samadhi,* the absolute goal of yoga – beyond total control of the mind.

When you understand how the different states of mind can be identified, and then derive from this the tools, techniques and practices needed to improve the current state, with the main goal being in the ultimate state, *niruddha,* meaning self-controlled and mindful, then you have the key, some may say the secret to coping with, benefiting from and growing because of change and not in spite of change.

Understanding the different states of mind, developing *Shraddha, Vivekah* and *Vairagya* will

41

ultimately make you more agile and accepting of inevitable change and will empower you and the business to inspire innovative performance.

And yet the world is so turbulent, it seems that there is little time for the luxury of these yogic concepts and the processes of personal development when so many businesses and organisations are fighting for survival. However, the danger is that dismissing or ignoring these concepts might mean that survival becomes less likely, not more.

We live and work in a world with a dominant mindset that says we can, and often must, control almost all forces, that everything is achievable and that power, will-power and single-minded determination will help achieve these goals. We are led to believe that all unknowns should be known, should be factored in, and on top of all that we have the old adage "if it ain't broke – don't fix it!" which assumes that whatever works now should be adhered to. The difficulty with this mindset is that it almost totally negates the inevitable change; transience, impermanence and flexibility, as well as understanding that acknowledging change can create anxiety and a feeling that you don't have control over the situation, leading to laid down patterns and habits of worry that failure or defeat may occur.

When a control-based mindset is prevalent in the leadership and management of any organisation, and you then view this mindset from a strategic perspective rather than from an immediate reactive one, it becomes obvious that those who tighten the reins around their own open views and fear thinking or acting "outside the box", as well as holding tight reins around their teams, may survive only if the system facilitates these more rigid views. However, the result is always the same and the team members lose their authenticity, their creativity and fluidity resulting in disharmony and discontent building up. There is no surer way to lose the most talented members, they feel squashed and will look elsewhere. The rigid (aka control freak) manager may remain but at a cost to the overall performance and wellbeing of the team and the organisation as a whole.

A great example of this is a man who headed a division in a large media company, whose style of leadership tended to be traditional and top-down. He had a reputation of being inflexible which created an element of dissatisfaction amongst his staff. One day he was involved in a car accident that resulted in a traumatic head injury and required extensive surgery. After a few months he returned to work, but gradually over time his once traditional leadership style became more and more chaotic and his decision-making more autocratic but less focused. He lacked clarity and he found it increasingly difficult to feel in control of his department.

He was referred for a course of interventions that included meditation and mindfulness. During that time not only did his general level of wellbeing and mental stability increase but his leadership style began to shift. He moved from being autocratic and controlling to being more open and tolerant of ideas. He encouraged differences in opinion and creative suggestions, he developed an ability to respond to situations rather than react to them and he approached the same situations as before with a less stressed and demanding attitude. It was replaced with one of openness to ideas, a willingness to guide rather than dictate, greater clarity and increased perspective. In his words, he was now able to bring a mindful approach to his style of leadership that was of benefit to him as a leader and to the creativity, decision-making skills and productivity of his whole department.

Resonance Vs Dissonance

To bring to a department or organisation the qualities of attention, focus and openness is certainly not a new idea, but what may be new is that the individual leader approaches the work environment with these qualities in order to promote resonance rather than dissonance amongst the team. Resonance is when the leader is able to draw out the qualities of others, hold them in mind and encourage their use. Such a leader approaches requirements by paying attention to what is happening around them and to what is required, and then flexibly aligns these components, even in difficult times, in an open and considered manner. Dissonance tends to occur when a leader insists on controlling the situation with rules and demands regardless of the wellbeing of the people and the organisation. Frequently, it is easier and less threatening to lead by demand, as the goals are set and the route to achievement predetermined.

Refusing to accept change will never work. All successful and thriving businesses must dare to deviate. As a leader, if you have the foresight to understand that change is inevitable, you can then encourage and build in sufficient resilience in individuals, teams and the organisation to manage then all from a resourceful and strengthened position.

To lead knowing that change is inevitable – though unpredictable in its timing – allows for flexibility, and a realisation that what worked in the past may not necessarily be appropriate today. This helps to safeguard an organisation from disillusionment and destruction because of enforced out-dated rules and processes.

The Benefits of Resilience

Developing and leading a resilient workforce will help:

- Reduce the cost of staff absenteeism caused by illness, injury and stress
- Improve cognitive functioning, memory, learning ability and creativity
- Improve productivity and improve overall staff and business wellbeing
- Reduce staff turnover and associated costs.

Understand that this is not a patronising fad implying that, if you are calm, everything will be fine. The reality of the working world is that all may not be fine. What being present, authentic, mindful and flexible can do is develop a thinking, emotional and instinctual mind so that as the leader you can do the best for yourself, your teams and the whole organisation.

TREND 2: Interdependence

An organisation works by people interacting: coming to work, doing things and talking to each other, having conversations about many different things (some of them to do with work!). You might give orders, make requests, ask questions, and discuss what to do and how to do it, debate strategy, produce marketing plans and so on.

Organisations as interactional systems

The way you talk is part of what shapes how events happen. And of course we talk in response to one another, which creates a network or you could also say a system-like feel: each response amplifies or dampens down the information conveyed by the previous speaker, to create looping, circular processes, this is a great way of understanding what interdependence is. Everything in an organisation is interdependent with everything else.

That is the key assumption of a systems approach. As managers of change, as great leaders you must be vigilant of any unnecessary blame for what is a much broader phenomena of the fear of change, be wary about attributing any blame to any one particular aspect. So even if someone says, "Oh, the leaders are causing the workforce to have low morale," that may be true, but the morale is also contributed to by the workforce and their morale affects the leadership as well, it's crucial to remain aware of this, as these links go in both directions.

"People are people through other people."

- Xhosa proverb

With this understanding of the interactional nature in organisations, usually the lower level is taken to be the individuals; the emergent properties at higher levels are the behaviours, relationships and results that those individuals generate in their interactions.

However much you know about each individual, about people in isolation, you can't accurately predict how they will interact. The whole cannot be reduced to the sum of the parts. The interaction has an apparent life of its own. If you want to change things, you can do so by helping any of the actors in the system to change their behaviour. This can only be done with their willing cooperation, because we assume that the individuals are basically capable of doing what they want to do, of functioning normally and productively. The action, if you want solutions, is in the interaction.

Discovering The Why

Willing cooperation comes from people when you can identify their values, their why... Why we do what we do? By identifying the why of clients, customers and anyone in the workforce is the how to get willing cooperation.

"People don't buy what you do, they buy why you do it."

- Simon Sinek

Simon, an author best known for popularizing the concept of "the golden circle", described by TED as "a simple but powerful model for inspirational leadership all starting with a golden circle and the question "Why?"'. (Wikipedia)

I saw Simon speak in 2011. His presentation was called "How great leaders inspire action"; its main message is that very few organisations know why they do what they do. Why they exist? Why should the CEO get out of bed in the morning?

By asking how some companies remain as innovative, leading edge leaders in their fields? Let's use Apple as an example, year after year; they always seem to lead innovation?

If you knew their secret, could you do it too?

It is actually easier than you might think, and the following information shows you how you too, can build a business fuelled on intelligence, innovation and inventiveness.

The Golden Circle in Simon's work – a simple model that provides you with the secret to being a great leader who inspires action. According to Simon inspired people and organisations all think, act, and communicate - from the inside out.

"Why" – in the centre,

Surrounded by "How",

Surrounded by a larger circle of, "What".

"People don't buy what you do; they buy why you do it."

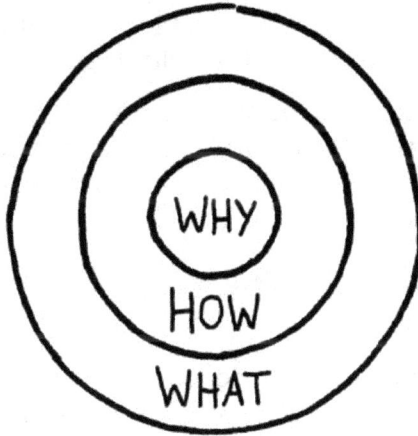

This model is grounded in biology. If you were to look at a cross section of the brain from top down, you'd see that it corresponds perfectly to the golden circle.

The Brain is The Golden Circle.

Starting at the top, our newest (in evolutionary terms) brain, Neocortex – it's our "What". It's responsible for all our rational, analytical thought, and language.

The middle two sections make up our limbic brain, which is for feelings, trust, and loyalty; it's also responsible for all human behaviour and decision making. It has no capacity for language.

So even though people can understand vast amounts of complicated information, features and benefits and facts and figures, it is not what drives behaviour.

When we communicate from the inside out, we're talking directly to the part of the brain that controls behaviour. This is where gut decisions come from. It's why you can give someone all the facts and figures and unless you connect to this feeling part of the brain it just doesn't 'feel' right and it won't be what they do.

Asking people "what" they do is usually easy for them to tell you, there are also some who know how they do it. But very very few people or organisations know WHY they do it.

Dharma – The Way.

The profits made are just the result. It's the "why", *Dharma* - why do you do it, why do you get out of bed in the morning, and why should people care.

If you don't know why you do what you do, then how will you ever get someone to buy into it, and be loyal, or to want to be a part of what it is that you do?

To create an inspired innovative workforce its not enough to get people to buy into your needs, they must to some extent share your beliefs. The goal is not just to hire people who need a job, but people who share your vision, your values and have faith in you and the business - *Dharma*.

We look at more depth into human needs in chapter 6, and for any further information about Simon Sinek his books and his work, use the CompaniesCanDoYogaToo.com website.

If you hire people who just need a job, they'll work for your money. But if you hire people that believe what you believe, they'll work for you with blood and sweat and tears.

And so we can see how Apple create fanatics out of followers – a cult if you will, of people who believe what you believe. They will stand in line all night to buy an iPad or the latest iPhone.

"People don't buy what you do, they buy why you do it. Because what you do, simply proves what you believe!" Simon Sinek.

People will do the things that prove what they believe.

Speaking to a value that they believed about themselves, this touches them in a way that they automatically want to connect to, to be connected. "People don't buy what you do, they buy why you do it."

There are leaders from previous paradigms who work with power and authority, and then there are those who lead in today's paradigm, those who inspire us. Whether within organisations or in all other areas of life, we follow those who lead, not because we have to, but because we want to. Not for them, but for ourselves.

Starting with why, gives you the ability to inspire those around you. Until an organisation identifies its central belief and message, it will not inspire the desired action.

Here is a golden circle I prepared for this book:

Dharma - The Purpose - WHY – Personally empower everyone of you in business to be a top performer in your chosen field, to grow within and contribute to your community and to society. Feel motivated, enthusiastic and empowered.

Jnana and Vairagya - The Process - HOW – Yoga, principles and practices, applies to all levels within the workplace, processes and practices.

Aishwarya - The Result - WHAT – People fulfil their potential, growing in confidence and self esteem, with improved leadership, great decisions, top results - personally and in terms of profits, inspired, authentic, creative, innovative, communicative, resilient, healthy and happy.

Now complete a golden circle for your company, maybe for your department too.

(It's also very interesting to do a personal one.)

How is interdependence a problem?

When you consider how people in your business relate to each other, to clients, to suppliers and customers, it is obvious that much has changed and evolved in recent years. Today relationships take place through many channels operating on many devices and for many reasons.

Some examples of how this may be reflected within your business are: Cross-Function or Departmental Work Groups, Matrixed Reporting Relationships, Geographically Dispersed Workforce and a heavy reliance upon Team-Based Work

Interdependence Demands Collaboration

While informal working relationships and networks have always been important, getting work done in the current working environment requires more collaboration among a broader and more diverse set of people than ever before. At the same time, the workforce is performing new tasks and working across more geographic locations. Collaborating today is more difficult to manage than it was yesterday and if you consider the growth of technology and the subsequent growth of numbers of people, resources and the amount of information that you have access to, you know that this shift will not slow down any time soon.

Looking at the charts below you can see how the rate of interdependence is impacting everybody in business. The information for these charts was supplied by both CEB and CLC for a Human Resources Survey.

This information is of great significance because of the sample size and distribution area from which it was collected.

Over 23,000 managers and employees across over 40 organisations globally were asked about the following changes over the past three years. (2009 – 2012)

Work requiring active collaboration

Decrease or no change 34%

Increase 66%

Number of co-workers in other geographic locations

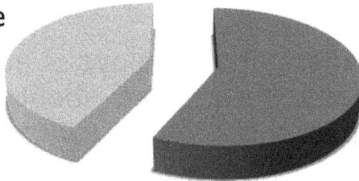

Decrease or no change 43%

Increase 57%

Number of people worked with on a day-to-day basis.

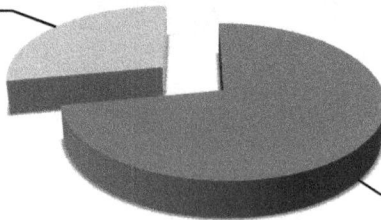

9 or less 28%

10 or more 72%

Manage external stakeholders.

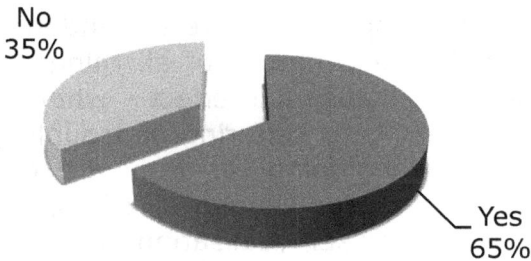

No
35%

Yes
65%

This data indicates very clearly how a modern workforce demands collaboration and how working with and through others further complicates the pace of workplace change. All of these changes disrupt employee networks and work processes, making connections hard to build and even harder to maintain.

Employees must navigate across different structures, cultures and processes to perform, but they struggle to understand whom to work with and how to work with them.

All this disruption and confusion is so stressful, and will often lead to a lack of ownership and accountability, an increase in blame and isolation among employees in the workforce, and it is a result of a lack of effective, objective leadership.

How do you make the workforce accountable and take ownership of what they do?

This question is a universal problem that you as an entrepreneur, a leader or a manager must manage efficiently and effectively and it is a growing phenomenon with ever increasing interdependence.

The Karmic Cycle

From a yogic perspective, interdependence can be described as the deep nature of all things, a concept known as Karma – cause and effect – where the cycles of conditions leading to suffering or trouble (*dukham*) are without any beginning, as they are cycles. Also understanding that even though all of us, as humans, have the capacity for self-realisation or enlightenment, we will not all achieve it and simply by stating that all things arise interdependently is not to affirm that they do so in a necessarily liberating way. Because although interdependence can mean increasing wealth, skilful means and happiness; It can also mean deepening poverty, trouble and suffering.

A big "Why" for so many of us to truly bring about the promise of expanded and deepened community in the context of increasing economic, social, political and cultural globalisation. This is dependent upon clearly discerning currently existing as well as emerging patterns of interdependence and consciously, intentionally focusing them in an empowering and liberating direction rather than toward suffering (*dukham*)

Ultimately, the promises of a global community and of deepening interdependence drive karma, the specific experiential force of intentions and values.

How the squirrel got its stripes

The following inspiring story is part of the great epic Indian Tale *Ramayana*.

56

It is said in Indian Folk law that the stripes on the back of the squirrel are for service to Lord Rama.

Lord Rama's wife Sita was abducted by the Demon King Ravana and kept in Lanka (meaning Island). The island Lanka, presently known as Sri Lanka, was ruled by the Mighty Demon Ravana; he was very powerful and dreaded by all. He committed many atrocities, and one among them was to kidnap and imprison beautiful women.

When Rama found out that Sita had been abducted, he began searching for her with the help of his friend Sugriva, a monkey king, and his army of monkeys. Eventually Rama found out that Sita was in Lanka, and to rescue her he had to go there, but it was an island off the mainland so to rescue her he had to cross the sea. The army of monkeys built a massive stone bridge. On each stone, Rama's name was chiselled and then thrown into the sea. Surprisingly, the stones did not sink but floated on the surface.

A squirrel watching all this was an ardent devotee of Lord Rama. She felt so sad that being so small, she could not help in building the bridge. She sat and contemplated her situation and, after thinking for some time, she made a decision. She went into the sands on the shores of the sea, rolled in it, went on to the bridge being constructed and shook the sand off. She went on rolling herself in the sand and then shaking off her body to deposit sand particles of sand amongst rocks brought by the monkeys.

When asked what she was doing, she said, "I am making my own small contribution to build the bridge for ending the injustice against Sita." The monkeys roared in mocking laughter: "We have never heard anything so foolish."

One day Lord Rama came to check the bridge, which was finished by now. He spotted the little squirrel and as he watched he became curious, so he went to her and asked what she was doing.

"I am making my own small contribution to build the bridge for ending the injustice against Sita." Hearing this, Lord Rama remarked, "Blessed be the little squirrel. You are doing your work to the best of your ability. You are as great as the greatest of this team of bridge builders."

The squirrel felt so happy seeing her lord before her eyes and how interested and grateful he was for her endeavours. She bowed at his feet and said, "O Rama, I am such a little creature. I love you so much but am not able to help you in any way. So I thought, if I cannot build this massive bridge, I can at least make the surface of the bridge soft for your delicate feet to tread on."

Rama was so touched by its service. He said "Dear squirrel, although you are small physically, your thoughts, your devotion and the service you are doing for me is so very great."

He took her into his hands and softly stroked her back. The squirrel lost her fatigue and became rejuvenated. Where Rama's hand ran along her back and as a remembrance of her service, he left the mark of three fingers, making three stripes running from head to tail. Rama said "from today, you and your species will carry this mark which will remind people of your great devotion and service."

The moral of this story is to never look down on those that are not as strong as you. What truly matters is not the strength you have, but the love and devotion with which you work.

True Collaboration

True collaboration is seeing the bigger picture, knowing the goal, being motivated even compelled to achieve the goal and, at the same time, being connected enough to know your role, to know how your role and your work play a crucial part *(dharma)*. Then, having knowledge of how to get the clearest picture of all that needs to be considered *(Jnana)*, how to progress *(vairagya)* and how to confirm when it is complete *(aishwariya)*.

Work collaboratively – high performers are good collaborators, working well with and through others.

58

They have the teamwork skills necessary to work with a wide range of people across the organisation. They use their technical expertise to influence stakeholders and contribute to collaborative projects.

"Success comes when people act together; failure tends to happen alone."

- Deepak Chopra

How to Achieve Collaboration

Collaboration will not occur unless organisations:

1. Enable and encourage broader employee networks – team building, socialising, openness, and easy access to information.

2. Connect employees as needed – provide simple and easy communication facilities.

3. Offer clear direction - objective, goal setting, (*Dharma*)

4. Provide appropriate technology – training and learning, (*Jnana*)

5. Support integrated workflow – doing the work with faith, (*Vairagya*)

6. Encourage aligned incentives – everyone gains, (*Aishwariya*).

Motivation is a force. It ignites, guides and maintains goal-oriented behaviour – causing us to take action, maybe to grab an umbrella when dark clouds are looming or perhaps to sign up for class to learn new skills. It can be biological, physical, metal, internal, external, social, emotional or even cognitive in nature.

In chapter 6 we explore the basic human needs that drive this force in more depth, but here let's simply understand the power of this force.

There are natural instincts and laws that affect us all. Whether we choose to acknowledge them and follow them is another story.

In the same way, people are motivated to behave in certain ways because they are evolutionarily programmed to do so. An example of this in the animal world is seasonal migration. These animals do not learn to do this, it is instead an inborn pattern of behaviour.

The Northern Wheatear is a tiny bird, a little bigger than a robin and weighs about 25 grams, that's about three pound coins. Each year it makes the most extreme migration known to man. This tiny insect-eating Arctic songbird, found throughout Alaska and the Canadian Arctic, is one of the tiniest birds to migrate. But the sheer scale of its yearly travels is staggering.

What is it that makes these tiny songbirds suddenly, one day, and especially when it's for the first time in its small life, decide to fly up to the natural current where it embarks on a 4,500 mile ride at 20,000 feet?

There are two populations of Wheatears, the western birds from eastern Canada leave their homes on Baffin Island and fly 2,000 miles to the British Isles in just four days. They then head south and fly another 2,500 miles to Mauritania in west African. It takes them just 26 days to make the trip south, and a relatively leisurely 55 days to get back to Baffin Island.

The eastern population, flying from Alaska, make the Canadian birds look like a bunch of wimps. They travel a whopping 9,000 miles each way every year.

To put this migration into perspective, we would have to travel roughly 50 million miles, proportionally speaking, to cover the same sort of distance. So, for us to migrate on the same scale as these tiny Arctic birds, our entire species would need to travel to Mars and back every single year.

The wheatear's migration patterns date back thousands of years, to a time trips long before humans even reached the Americas. In all those thousands of years, the birds have apparently never decided to just stay in the Arctic for the winter, or even settle on a shorter journey to the warmer parts of the Americas. To me this shows that the power of natural law is beyond our imagination, strong enough to drive these birds to keep on making this journey year after year after year. The Wheatear has no idea why it does it, it just knows it has to be done, it's natural Law.

Motivation - the Fruit of Collaboration

How can you attract and keep an employee like the tiny wheatear or the little squirrel? A true high performer, dedicated, motivated, ready to do anything, stretch to any level to contribute their best. A motivated workforce will inherently create a sense of ownership and accountability for the desired results so the job of getting results gets done.

Aishwariya means prosperity and wealth, but more than the material aspects of these words, there are the feelings that go with this state, this attitude, think self-confident, open hearted, celebrating and blissing out on existence!

*"It is the long history of humankind
(and animal kind, too) those
who learned to collaborate and
improvise most effectively have prevailed."*

- Charles Darwin

10 Steps to Ownership and Accountability

1   Develop a personal connection.

If you know, understand and appreciate each person's strengths and weaknesses, you can encourage ownership by developing trust and maintaining a positive attitude with them.

2   Clarify each person's responsibility.

Through effective delegation everyone will know the desired outcomes, what challenges they must meet and what work they must take ownership of.

3   Ensure proper training and equipment.

This enables everyone to perform their work so they will feel prepared to succeed. Make it clear that you want all of them to be successful.

4   Empowerment through autonomy.

Make sure that all are empowered with the authority and information they need to make decisions that affect their own performance.

5   Key Practice Involvement.

Include people in goal-setting, planning, and implementing change. That way they can take ownership of decisions that affect them.

6   Practice Deep Listening.

Always listen to employees. When problems emerge, encourage participation, new ideas, and ownership of solutions.

7   Practice and encourage openness

Sharing organisational goals, plans and performance feedback means every one can see the bigger picture, encouraging openness and authenticity.

8   Reward desired performance.

Rewards and incentives demonstrate that there are good reasons to take ownership of their performance and a desire to contribute.

9   Provide opportunities for growth.

Being able to gain new skills and talents means, everyone grows and there is something in this for everyone. Encourages people to be more committed to both the job and the organisation.

10   Celebrate success

Understanding the importance of celebration success. We all want to feel part of a winning enterprise and because being successful and recognised as such makes it much more desirable for people to come to work. Recognition of strong performance increases the desire for more.

Following these steps will help you create a workplace that brings out the best in the entire workforce, while at the same time increasing their ownership and creating accountability. This will naturally result in the development of effective systems and processes that improve performance.

Great leadership creates an environment in which employees have a sense of ownership in any activity they engage in. When done well, accountability becomes a habit *(samskara)* *and Aishwariya* – jubilation automatically follows.

Motivation is a means to get people to buy in and take ownership of the organisation's needs as well as their own engagement.

A) Increase ownership of performance and

B) Create accountability for results.

With clear responsibilities and goals, and well established standards of performance that are challenging yet realistic, you will encourage and motivate people. Giving balanced and on-going performance feedback means everyone is aware of how well they are performing and where additional coaching or training needs are too.

By identifying ways to improve, recognise and reinforce desired levels of performance, any need to deal with issues that are damaging group performance and morale can be identified and rectified fairly and openly. Social proof has a very deep impact on the individuals in any group and enhances the collaborative behaviours that support the buy-in and accountability needed in the interdependent structures we all will thrive in.

TREND 3: Knowledge workers

In the workplace today we see exponential growth in the quantity and complexity of information and data. Gazillions of terabytes of the stuff! This is the result of the ready availability of ever expanding computing power, proliferation of business applications, more process automation, and increased outsourcing of routine work.

As a result, most work processes are highly automated, and work in general has become more data and information intensive, which in practical terms means less routine and more "exceptions" based.

Who is a Knowledge Based Worker?

Working with data and information has become the core of most people' jobs, with over seventy-five percent reporting a significant increase in time spent working with data and information. (Data from CLC Human Resources High Performance Survey)

While definitions vary, more and more employees are knowledge workers – anyone who collects, manages, uses, analyses and makes decisions using information as a primary part of his or her day-to-day job is a knowledge based worker. Almost three out of four executives report that more than half of their staff are now knowledge workers.

Unfortunately, not everyone has achieved proficiency in being able to find information, analyse it and use sound business judgment to make decisions.

There is a need for expert knowledge workers, those with the ability to effectively analyse information to make sound decisions. On average, less than forty per cent of employees actually fall into the category.

Expert Decision Makers

The best decision makers are found at the executive level, and the number of workers with the right balance of skills declines rapidly at lower levels in the organisation.

And yet today almost everyone is a knowledge worker. Since knowledge work requires both ready access to the right information and effective decision making with that information, organisations need to ensure that employees have the right skills and abilities to use advanced information technology effectively in their jobs.

Even though most business currently operate through a web of collaborating knowledge workers. Employees in this environment have more ambiguous objectives, and their work is interconnected with a growing, more dispersed network.

Choosing Between Right and Right.

How to choose between right and right and make effective decisions?

Mahatma Gandhi based his life on two fundamental principles:

Satya - (unconditional adherence to the truth) and

Ahimsa – (unreserved practice of nonviolence in thought, speech and deed).

These two principles are also the first two *yamas*, in the first step of Patanjali's *Astanga*, chapter 5.

One day a journalist remarked to Gandhi that, in some cases, telling the truth could actually cause harm to others. Gandhi asked for an

67

example. The journalist then related a carefully crafted spiritual dilemma for the Mahatma to solve:

"A monk was sitting peacefully at a crossroad. A noise attracted his attention and, as he looked up, a wounded deer galloped past and took one of the roads leading away from the intersection. A few minutes after the deer had disappeared a hunter came to where the monk was still sitting. He cast about him but couldn't determine which way the beast had fled, so he asked the monk if he could point him in the right direction."

Gandhi smiled knowingly the dilemma the monk was facing.

The journalist continued, "If the monk answered 'yes', he was compromising his vow of *ahimsa*, because he would become the material cause of the deer's death. But if he said 'no', he was compromising *Satya* by resorting to lying."

Looking the Mahatma straight in the eye, the journalist asked the crucial question. "Gandhiji, what should the monk answer?"

"Let me answer your clever scenario by a story. It comes from one of the scriptures composed by Sage Vyasa, the Devi Bhagavata."

Mahatma Gandhi fixed his gaze in a distant horizon and started. "Sage Satyavrata had taken the vow of always saying the truth – hence his name (Vow of Truth). One day he saw, running towards him, a pig that had been struck by an arrow. It stopped, looked about it and then hid in the bushes nearby. Soon a fierce-looking hunter came and asked Satyavrata whether he had seen a pig wounded by an arrow. Satyavrata gave an answer which saved the pig, *dharma*, and possibly his own life."

What was it?

Mahatma Gandhi explained, "Very calmly, Sage Satyavrata said, 'My eyes have seen but they cannot speak. My mouth can speak but it cannot see. Please leave me in peace, Oh hunter, and go your way.'

The hunter was so impressed by the courage of this answer that he begged apology and left."

Turning to the journalist, Mahatma Gandhi concluded, "Most importantly, know that if anybody asks a question, one is never obliged to give an answer."

This is a crucial point to remember: no one is ever required to tell everything, or to answer every question, if it might cause harm to the innocent. In other words, non-injury must always supersede truth-telling.

Blind Truth is No Truth

Ahimsa is the golden rule found in many different guises in all religions: "Do no harm".

A story from the *Puranas* (tales of Indian folk law) confirms this principle.

A much-respected sage had once blindly adhered to telling the truth, thereby causing the death of hundreds of innocent people. When he died years later, despite his vehement protests that he was a man who had always defended the truth, he was taken to Hell.

The angel of death warned him, "By making truth a blind principle, you walked away from the path of compassion, and this is what led you here."

Applying sound judgment makes good business decisions and employees are making more business decisions much lower in the organisation. They need more high-quality information and tools to make those decisions. But most of all, they need the experience and skills to apply sound judgment in decision making.

For an organisation to thrive it needs a different kind of employee, one that is immune to the paralysing complexities of change, willing to collaborate with a broad range of individuals and able to apply judgment in an increasingly knowledge-based role.

While hiring new staff with stronger aptitude in the new core skills will help over time, there is no substitute for experience. The competencies essential to strong performance are best developed through on-the-job experience with a single company over time.

Are you recruiting the right people?

More importantly are you developing, training and retaining them?

"Employees are a company's greatest asset - they're your competitive advantage.
You want to attract and retain the best; provide them with encouragement, stimulus, and make them feel that they are an integral part of the company's mission."

- Anne M. Mulcahy

Chapter 3

How will Yoga Benefit Your Business?

As a business focused solution model, yoga will benefit the three key components of your business

1. The People – developing and sustaining physical and mental resilience.
2. The Leaders – developing inspiring, innovative and authentic strategists and managers.
3. Organisation – delivering successful growth, dynamic and leading edge processes, expanding top line revenues and bottom line profits.

What is yoga?

Yoga has so many definitions; the most authentic, the classical, the original, is given clearly in the Yoga Sutras of Patanjali, a relatively short (196 lines) but dense and complex text, written in a language called Sanskrit, and containing knowledge that can be dated back as far as 5000 years (a conservative estimation).

"Yoga Citta Vritti Nirodaha"

Yoga is - when the activity (*vritti*) of the mind *(citta)* is stopped (*nirodaha).*

The next sutras go on to tell us that in this state the mind (*citta*) becomes like pure crystal – reflecting equally and without distortion, the perceiver, the perception and the perceived.

Yoga is when the activity of the mind is stopped. A simple enough statement, but what does it mean? And why bother?

What is *citta*?

Citta is a Sanskrit concept meaning the mind stuff (very technical!) or the personality complex: made up of the unconscious and subconscious mind and all the mind-stuff, like the signals that the senses bring, it's here where memories, habits, tendencies and thought patterns are found. It is derived from the root *chit*, "to be conscious".

The stopping Patanjali talks of is *nirodaha*, or the cessation of perception and feeling. It can be compared to the "no mind" of Buddhist meditation. As with most Sanskrit words and concepts, it is difficult to translate. It can be said to mean that You, the observer, your real authentic conscious aware Self, is able to observe and distinguish between right knowledge and wrong knowledge, and distinguish the real knowledge, be it based on words or logic and reasoning or sensory perceptions, so that all this knowledge no longer runs around in the mind in a mixed-up state.

This mixed-up state is our usual state and is the sum total of all of the mind's activity – *Citta Vrittis*; meaning mental whirlwinds, which seem to leave no room for anything else!

But how can stopping the mind benefit you or your business?

You are a Diamond

Yoga is very deep and complex, so I hope you'll enjoy going down this rabbit hole with me!

Down the rabbit hole, to find your crystal – the bright diamond within yourself, at your very centre, which, when it shines out, spreads light and understanding before you, all around you, giving pure clear perception that expands and transforms how you live, love and work, how you lead and parent, how you play, how you innovate, create and manage and so expands and transforms, by default, automatically and inevitably, how you grow and how you profit.

The purpose of yoga?

To attain liberation from all pain and misery.

The foundation of all six of the Indian philosophies, including yoga, has this liberation as the goal – to move away from *dukham* – stress, and go on a journey towards *Sukham*- happiness.

There is one particular yoga sutra in Chapter II of Patanjali's Yoga Sutras, in which he tells how and why we encounter misery and pain (*dukham)*

Dukha can also be translated as: out of balance, out of sync, stressed, discomfort, closed heart, hard heart, a feeling of emptiness.

What you **don't** want is...

>   Duh = constriction, closed, hard.

>   Kham = space within the heart.

What you **do** want is...

>   Sukham = balance, clarity.

>   Suk = expansive, open, comfort, joy.

>   Kham = space within the heart.

Dukha is identified as existing because of three factors in Patanjali's Yoga Sutra II:15:

1. *Parinama* = Change, both internal and external (requires acceptance, being present and compassion)
2. *Tapa* = desire/thirst (burning obsessive desire and can be resolved by *Tapas* control of all physical actions = self discipline)
3. *Samskara* = Habit, tendency (a process held at a *VijnanaMayaKosha* level)

Unless these three factors are perfectly aligned then there is *dukham* (pain).

*"If you are depressed
you are living in the past.
If you are anxious
you are living in the future.
If you are at peace
you are living in the present."*

- Lao Tzu

Not All Change is Painful

Parinama – change is constant and everything is constantly changing! From the quantum perspective it is clearly understood what this means. From a yogic perspective the only thing not changing is the observer.

This one fact alone causes so much pain and suffering for us; when we like something we don't want it to change, we hate change, the idea of change causes us to display very imbalanced behaviours. Often our behaviour is so automatic we call it unconscious; it is as if invisible to us.

Instead we look outside where we want to control the environment we are in (over which we have very little power), we insist on forming great big high expectations based on external factors and without accounting for change, waiting with all the "if only he'd . . . (*fill in the blank)* then I'd be happy and we could live happily ever after", so we hate change.

By thinking in this way we are giving up our power, and it's a choice. Not one that we are taught in school, we are given and continue to make many assumptions that it is true, that we can control and change the external world around us, but it is merely a belief and absolutely not true. We do have a choice, and it starts with taking responsibility for ourselves rather than being the victim of circumstance. This victimhood is a huge get-out-clause for being responsible (unless, that is, the change brings us exactly what we need to become happy, like a big huge dose of self-love, the spiritual kind, not the closed-fist kind! A dose of compassion, and if not...) and because we are searching for love and happiness outside of ourselves we persist in a state of perpetual disappointment rejecting our own responsibility – and we perceive change as robbing us of what we love, because we judge things as they are in the image in our mind and not how they'll become in the present, in reality. We are masters of the big disappoint!

*"Some changes look negative on the surface
but you will soon realise that
space is being created in your life
for something new to emerge."*

— Eckhart Tolle

To Be or Not To Be – You Choose

It's such a shame that we don't take advantage of our own inherent changing, this constant changing that has always been going on and yet somehow we miss it. We remember snapshots, stuck in a time warp of disappointment; not seeing the reality of the situation but instead waiting for it to get better so we can feel better.

Yoga teaches a shortcut to getting better and feeling happier. Don't wait for the thing, because actually it's not the thing at all – there is no magic pill, no magic asana that will change your feelings, rather, you have to do it yourself. You have to choose, to find yourself in your 'happy place' and learn to re-create the feeling, not how to recreate the environment as it is in that split second.

Yoga teaches you how to transform your life through patient, diligent, disciplined practice (known as *Tapas*). You gain experiences that transform actions moment by moment, transform how you experience your life. By connecting to the body, internally, feeling the sensations, the temperature, and the pressure. Feel your left foot right now, is it squashed up in a shoe, is it cosy and comfy? Is it warm or cold?

Become more aware of your body, finding your "why" – your *dharma,* from the inside, because it's only through contacting your body and feeling how life is that you can come to know the truth of who you are – the witness, the observer, the conscious Self.

The Oldest Matryoshka

Matryoshka is a Russian doll – you know the ones that can be separated into two parts and inside is a smaller one – then another smaller one inside that until you have a teeny tiny one...

I want to use this to introduce the next part of yoga's brilliance to you; The *Pancha Koshas* or 5 envelopes, sheaths or layers.

Yoga offers such a broad range of benefits, because it works holistically on all levels of our being, not just the physical body. According to yoga philosophy, we are not just our physical body or mind, we are holistic, multi-dimensional beings made up by many different, interactive levels.

The concepts that underpin modern Yoga have come from ancient ideas and practices given to us by *Rishis* (teachers or seers) and have been handed down to us today in various forms both verbal and written. The Taittiriya Upanishad is third amongst a set of the very oldest texts that explain the concept of the five sheaths or *kosha*.

To understand the five sheaths or *pancha kosha* using the Matryoshka idea, each embedded within the others. Starting from the outermost layer and moving towards the core, the *pancha kosha* proceed from outer, gross level to inner and becoming more and more subtle as you move in:

All models of course have their limitations, as does this one, yet still it can help to separate out the different aspects or strands that make up the human being, to facilitate the development of discriminatory wisdom *Vivekah* and detachment *Vairagya*. The levels are affected in varying ways by all life-style habits, by thoughts, beliefs and emotions and, of course, by the different yogic practices we will illustrate later in this book.

The fourth *kosha* is the emotional body (*VijnanaMayaKosha*). Learning how to play with it will give you back your power, so you can enjoy life as an experience that naturally has the ups and the downs, enjoy the struggles, see the lessons in the pain, see the growth within the suffering and be set free from pain.

Yoga is a wealth of tools and techniques, movements, shapes, sounds and breaths . . . big ones! There are so many tools and techniques and they are systematic, scientific, tried and tested and tested again. Can you imagine before TV, cinema, electricity, before all of these and more of the things that we think of as attractions, or should I say distractions? No wonder we've lost touch with our bodies – there is just so much technology humming away and attracting our attention!

My study of yoga has brought me to a place where I can see it is possible to always enjoy life, whatever happens, that you can always "put your glad rags on and let's go party!" Letting go of any attachments to the past, to the expectation it wouldn't, shouldn't, couldn't change, and allow the change to be a positive one within – because the environment within is what we do have control over, that's where our real power is. Fuelled by *yogachara* (a yogic lifestyle), good food, good thoughts, good company and role models, good fun and relaxation and, most importantly, celebration.

Let's Celebrate And Have A Yoga Party

With the right ingredients from *yogachara, Tapa* or burning obsessive desire, can become an instrument to assist in nurturing acceptance, developing new habits, new beliefs, ones that truly serve you, reflecting the reality of your existence, through awareness placed firmly on the object of your desire. Celebrating all of life, with all of your five bodies; now that's what I call good science! Dancing with all the *pancha Koshas* aligned, accepting what is and nurturing the internal Self, not the external personality.

When the external personality melts away, then the true light of the spirit shines out for all to see, the Self is available for all to witness and share.

The mind is part of the personality, sometimes referred to as the ego, and is very stubborn. It seems the more we study and learn, the more intelligence we have, the more knowledge we have, then the more important the mind thinks it is and it becomes hungrier and hungrier for more!

This means it's impossible to satisfy the mind, because there will always be more, more to do, more to learn! But while the mind is so easily distracted by the senses, and while the external mask of the personality is drawn out, we can never experience *sukham*, the bliss that exists in just being the Self and the beauty and radiance of our spirit shining forth.

Because we focus on the external parts of life, pain and suffering are inevitable. So much suffering! If you consider something as drastic as plastic surgery, it seems like a self-activity, but actually the witnessing Self is untouched. This type of activity is an extreme expression of this basic cultural belief that gets deep into the core of the mind – that old is bad, young is good, fat is bad, thin is good, who wants to be saggy and haggy and old or fatty and batty?! But the nature of this very universe and everything in it is changing, constantly, incessantly. Time marches on and the Self just witnesses.

We must come to understand this constant change *Parinama*, in our environment, in our mood, in our state of mind, in our communities, in our work, and begin to learn how to accept it. Learn how to play along with the emotional rollercoaster of life and at the same time feel that deep stable sense of the inner consciousness that we are. At this fundamental level the Self, separate from the emotions, can witness the emotions and at the same time, remain centred, aligned and witnessing – this is the goal of yoga.

"The primary cause of unhappiness is never the situation but your thoughts about it."

— Eckhart Tolle

We are trapped inside our own heads. To come out of your old habits, to emerge from your old state of mind, in order to transform we must undergo some pain, mental and physical. Mentally we are emotionally involved in, and want to hold onto, our beliefs, which are part and parcel of our habitual thinking processes – *samskara*.

So in order to transform we must get rid of *samskara,* old beliefs, old habits, old feelings, old thought patterns, old neural pathways. *Tapa* is like a fire used by the alchemist to burn away the dross of the past and deliver a pure nugget of gold that exists in this present moment. The objective is to purify (by rewriting those neural pathways) our physical actions, thoughts and feelings so we can surrender to universal law, truth and love, which will nourish us and take us gracefully toward the state of *sukham*.

Re-wiring Your Brain

A belief is just a repeated thought, it is implied that if we believe in something then it is not a truth, so we don't say we believe the sun rises in the east, rather, it simply does; we don't have to believe the leaves will fall from the tress, they just do. A belief is an assumption either that we have made using our own logic and reasoning or it had been handed to us by an authority figure, by our society or our community.

Beliefs can cloud our mind so much that even the simplest task seems daunting or perhaps impossible, if the mind is overwhelmed by information, opinions, judgements, likes and dislikes then life will be a struggle. We all have our own individual habits and patterns of thoughts and behaviours, *samskara* and we tend toward the same patterns over and over; they may be a wide variety of behavioural, emotional, thinking patterns – this is part of what forms the mask of personality, the *citta*.

Your state of mind must be aligned to your current activity in order to be successful, so when you are trying to sleep the mind must be peaceful or you won't sleep. Disturbances and imbalances happen in the mind when the state of mind not aligned with the activity it sets as its current goal. This is why you have *Dukha*.

To understand a little more of the primordial forces of suffering, and how it arises I will share with you a little more yoga philosophical concepts of the mind.

The Three Gunas

There are three *Gunas* or basic states of matter:

1. *Sattva* – Balanced – great for doing exams, making considered decisions, goal setting

2. *Rajas* – Active – good for driving, getting out of stressful situations

3. *Tamas* – Dull – good for resting and sleeping

When the mind is in any one of or any combination of these states then the body will follow. Later we can see how these *gunas* play a role in the states of mind.

The goal of yoga is to reach a *sattvic* state, through purification of the body, the senses and the mind. This will be achieved by following and practicing *yogachara*, as described in chapter 5. Then you will be in harmony with the natural rhythms of life, by carefully adjusting your lifestyle, routines, diet, physical and mental exercises.

I hope you have enjoyed our first excursion down into the rabbit hole, and delving a little deeper into the concepts, systems and models that have been used to build the brilliant body of work known as Patanjali's yoga sutras, which can be used as a handbook to a happier more fulfilled life.

All of my subsequent studies since I learned of this great work have always lead me back to the Yoga Sutras, because even though they are seemingly short, they do seem to contain all the wisdom needed to get through life and I have always been able to find one or more of the sutras to help me understand even more deeply all of my subsequent learning.

As a huge fan of Patanjali, I have studied the yoga sutras under many masterful teachers and just this one sutra, from chapter II line 15 comes up again and again. It has been a great turning point in my understanding of me, of who I am and who I'm not and how to live a happier and healthier life in harmony with all around me.

Parinama tapa samskara duhkaih gunavrtti virodhat ca duhkham eva sarvam vivekinah.
Yoga Sutra II:15

1. Parinama – change.
2. Tapa – desire.
3. Samskara – Habit.

4. Duhkaih – Pain/sorrow
5. Gunavrtti – Naturally changing states of mind and matter
6. Virodhat – Opposing/conflicting
7. Sarvam - All
8. Vivekinah – The wise one

A wise, discriminating person sees all worldly experiences as painful, because of reasoning that all these experiences lead to more consequences, anxiety, and deep habits, as well as acting in opposition to or conflicting with the natural qualities of nature, constant change.

Breath is the Bridge from Body to Mind

The breath acts as the bridge between the body and the mind.

What is your breath doing now? Take a few seconds to check in with your breath:

Is it slow or fast?

Is it deep or shallow?

Is your belly moving?

Is your back moving?

Is your ribcage moving?

Is there any noise?

Is there any gap after inhaling – before the exhale starts?

Is there any gap after exhaling – before inhale starts?

Breathing needs to happen in a way that also supports the current goal, and a balanced and calm breath never engages the ribcage – if you watch a baby, or a yogi, breathing when at rest then you see the whole body expand as they breathe in, the belly rises, this is like the start of the wave that is the inhalation.

Now with this calm mind and body let's delve a little deeper down our rabbit hole...

Mindless Yoga – The Best There Is!

> *"All true artists, whether they know it or not, create from a place of no-mind, from inner stillness."*
>
> — Eckhart Tolle

You may have heard of "No mind" (or maybe not), it is a term sometimes given to a state of deep meditation. In this state of no mind, the first thing you come to know is that thoughts are like clouds – they come and go – and you, you are the sky.

When there is no mind you immediately realise that you are not actually involved in the thoughts, because the thoughts are there passing through you, like clouds passing through the sky, or the wind passing through the trees, like a film passing across a screen. The thoughts are there, passing through you and they can pass through easily because you are a "vast emptiness" or "Wast emptiness" as Osho so poetically says – there is nothing in their way, no hindrance, no obstacle.

Thoughts come and go and once you realise this and that you are the watcher, the witness, the observer, in that moment of realisation, the mind is under control. This is yoga.

Osho and many other sources of wisdom I have learned from are listed on the website of the book – with some cool links to help to further expand some of the ideas I am sharing in this book.

Who exactly is in control here?

The mind is never actually under control in the first place, it can't be if doesn't exist.

"What do you mean doesn't exist!"

The mind is an event, it's not a thing- it's a happening, so you can't control it? Because nobody exists beyond the mind there is just nothingness – infinite empty sky.

So who controls the mind?

If somebody seems to be controlling the mind it is just a part of the mind controlling another figment of the mind. The thoughts are the clouds, the puppets and it's all a crazy puppet show!

So who is asking these questions?

A part of your mind...

Who is answering? – Another part of the same mind!

This controlling figment of the mind is the ego (*asmita*). The mind cannot really be controlled in that way, by itself, because it is not... and there is nobody to control it. The inner emptiness, the observer, can see but cannot control. It can look but not control, and then when this ability to look is achieved; the look is the control, the phenomena of observation becomes the control because the mind disappears. If you imagine for a moment on a dark night you are running fast because you got scared thinking someone is following, but that somebody is your own shadow, so the more you run, the faster you run the closer the shadow gets.

So then after lots of scared running you become quite exhausted and it doesn't seem to matter how fast you run, the shadow is still there right next to you. Running is not the way to escape from it or control it. Instead you must just look deeper into the shadow, stand still, and suddenly you'll realise it's not anything, it is just the absence of light, a shadow doesn't exist, can't exist when there is light.

In the same way, the mind is nothing but the absence of your own presence. When you sit in silence, silently looking deep into the mind, the mind simply disappears. Thoughts remain – they are existential, they exist – but the mind will not be found.

"Why do you stay in prison when the door is so wide open? Move outside the tangle of fear-thinking. Live in silence."

-Rumi

The thoughts have some substance, an energy, a field, and mind is like a flock of thoughts

Imagine a flock of starlings, a huge, orchestral, choreographed, swooping, swirling and diving dense dark cloud over the sea or over the reed beds of the UK on an autumnal evening. The dark forms and shapes that they make in the sky appear to be real things – the flock, this is like the mind, it's composed of the constant and incessant thoughts, *vrittis,* whirlwinds... like the starlings within the flock, but meditation, *pranayama* and *asana* all help to develop a quieter mind, slowing down the pace of the thoughts, finding the space in-between the thoughts and experiencing this space as clear of thought... without a trace – just as the darkening dusk skies become clear when the flocks of birds leave it without trace.

When You look deeply, the mind is controlled and suddenly you have become the master. The thoughts are still there but they are no longer the master, You are. They can't do anything to You, they just come and go but You remain untouched like sky.

The hugely significant symbol of the lotus flower is used to help understand this, because like a lotus flower in the rain, as the drops of rainfall onto the petals, the petals remain as if untouched. Be like a lotus – so symbolic of Eastern consciousness, untouched by thoughts, remain untouched and You are in control.

There is only acceptance of what is and choice of how you respond to what is.

With this as your new perspective You suddenly realise You are in control and it is an empowered position of strength, it is *aishwariya*.

Chapter 4

My story

I worked for over 20 years in the IT "industry", I went from technical programming, as a software engineer to project management and quality management. During this time I worked for many diverse types of organisation, like banks, insurance, telecommunications and on many different projects. At the same time I was self-employed and running my own small business too.

Even though I enjoyed the work, I was allowed to express my creativity as I designed and created software and able to develop and grow my people skills as a client facing team co-ordinator and test manager. However I was usually desk bound and the internal politics, unnecessary competitiveness, blame culture and lack of collaboration caused me much stress and encouraged dis-satisfaction.

I did not address this stress and as a result I was diagnosed in 1996 with an auto-immune hypothyroid condition, I began taking medication which managed some of the symptoms; but after 10 years the medication was now taking it's toll on my body... I developed double vision, and an inflammatory condition that was associated with original diagnosis.

Around this time, 2006, I decided I wanted to teach yoga. This may seem to you like a huge jump... but I had been attending yoga classes for many years by this time. My first yoga class was in 1990, I couldn't find an aerobics class, I tried it as a substitute for aerobics and just loved it.

I'd never really experienced that quality of peace of mind it gave me. It took me a year or so to work out that's what it was that kept drawing me back. It was this great sense of peace of mind, the slowing down of thoughts, the engagement with the present. Very profound and very subtle at the same time.

During my IT days I was travelling a lot and although my work wasn't always completely satisfying me, it was paying me well, well enough to travel, a lot, and on longer and longer trips, enjoying many fascinating adventures. I spent a couple of years in Mexico and I had an opportunity to help out in a gym, a really lovely gym with huge windows on two sides, looking out onto the rich turquoise of the Caribbean Sea. It was so beautiful. There had been a friendly couple managing this gym but one sunny morning, they disappeared! Later I found out Interpol were involved... their five children had been from two separate marriages (no one knew) and they'd taken the kids out of the country without telling the other partners.

My roommate Lynda was the aerobics teacher and personal trainer at the gym, that day she found herself the only member of staff, alone and in charge, a great opportunity for me to help out. I began running a daily yoga club in the mornings and very soon could clearly hear my heart.. "This is what I've got to do."

I was hooked, I loved teaching yoga, I felt amazing through the regular practice it gave me and in awe of the unbelievable transformations happening with the students I was helping. I knew with every fibre of my body that this was want I wanted to do. So I went to live in India for a couple of years and trained as a yoga teacher and therapist. I learned loads about yoga philosophy and the theory, as well as the practice. And I discovered the power of yoga as a form of healing and how it helps you to achieve peak performance both mentally and physically.

From my many years in business I have a deep understanding that the people are the most important thing in a business. Those people might be the workers, they might be the leaders and they might be the clients. My experience has been that by looking after people as individuals and working with them first, you will automatically influence the whole organisation.

As a result I have developed and work with a business growth solution called The P R I M E Profit Paradigm™ to instruct and coach people who become the builders, the workforce and the supporters of brilliant businesses.

This new paradigm will bring you out of the dinosaur industrial age and into the current technology driven digital age. This system is a pathway to getting there cleanly and being able to grow confidently. The vehicle I use is Yoga.

If I ask you to make a list of what stresses you out, I'm sure you can do a list as long as your leg. If I ask you what you do to replenish and relax? I know that there are some who can't think of even one thing. Yoga helps you have two lists that are a bit more balanced, more harmonious.

I have a number of colleagues who work in coaching and training, we have become aware of the huge gap in businesses at the moment, a gap between their planned goals and objectives and those actually achieved. Fear prevents growth, because most people are too scared to step outside of what feels comfortable, afraid to get out of the box of sameness and into the new, the unknown, so even though there are new plans, perhaps great progressive five or ten year plans, they stay as unrealised dreams. Instead those plans that are realised are either really short term or have a very narrow focus.

In order to bridge that gap to bring this next level of evolution to a business where you're confident to grow, then you need to have a different mindset.

The M of "P R I M E" is for mindset and more specifically mindset alignment. Again, using different yoga concepts you'll be inspired as we work on the difference between ignorance and wisdom. Not ignorance because of lack of education but ignorance because you don't know. You don't realise what the truth is of all these beliefs that they're not actually the truth. A belief is just a repeated thought and as such can be changed.

I have also learned how powerful it is to use breathing and breath awareness to connect to the brain, to switch on the brain circuitry to get the body out of fear so that the brainpower is actually maximised. My background is very science based and I have explored lots of neuroscience and psychology that supports this understanding and practice too.

I trained to teach yoga at "The Yoga Institute" in Mumbai, the oldest organised yoga school in the world. A Raja yoga school, which is the yoga of kings. It's about mediating and really getting to grips with the knowledge that comes when you meditate, about the cleaning of the mind needed to reach the level of meditation at which that knowledge is apparent, at which we transcend old ways of being.

I also trained at the "KYM", a very famous school in Chennai. Here I learnt a lot more about teaching one to one and doing yoga therapy. That's like personal training with yoga, healing and coaching, all rolled into one.

I loved all the Sanskrit studies that were available in India and I did lots at both schools. The main focus being Patajalis' yoga sutras – that's like the yoga bible. He's amazing. This ancient wisdom is so mind-blowing! His knowledge is so brilliant - even now with the contemporary technology we have – active functional magnetic resonance style brain scans and neuroscience and quantum physics – his stuff is absolutely spot on and you can marry it in with so much of the psychology, neuroscience, science and technology of today, it is accurate and clarifies so much stuff.

My own journey continued, and even though I had been diagnosed with thyroid eye disease, I decided not to accept all the surgeries and medical treatment offered to me. I had faith in the body's ability to heal itself. On my own healing journey I have discovered and trained in a number of modalities and processes that combine many areas of ancient wisdom and cutting edge science, energy psychology and META-Medicine, this is a method of understanding the behaviour of tissues in the body based upon the assumption 'The body does not make mistakes'. This offers a way to determine the root cause, the behaviours, emotions and beliefs from which symptoms merge at a tissue level. Now understanding this I have identified it was my behaviours, my beliefs and my emotional patters that informed my body to behave in this way.

My condition was a result of my conditioning. I was brought up in a very violent house, there was alcoholism, lots of aggression, a lot of physical violence. I had to "seek external approval" and "keep an eye out for danger!" So my body did just that, it grew in a modified way and pushed one of my eyes out of my head – the perfect solution to the needing to be on constant and vigilant alert, on the lookout for danger.

Now with this new way of understanding my organism and it's behaviour I'm slowly but surely reversing all this life long and constant worry and fear. Nobody knew. It wasn't apparent. It was so subliminal and so subtle, running through all aspects of me – outwardly I'm such a confident, outgoing character. People were never aware of this fear and this worry that was a constant background aspect, like background noise, to me. Even I wasn't aware of it because that was my life. It was constant and unconscious. Now I understand that more deeply.

I'm working on slowing down and being receptive rather than going out constantly looking for information. I'm in a safe place now. I can sit back and let the information come to me and then decide what to do about it.

My condition has been monitored constantly by a team at London's Moorefield's Eye Hospital who have been amazing. At my last visit I was told many of my symptoms have reduced and some reversed. When I asked how they viewed this, I was told that they'd call it spontaneous remission. "But doctor! 5 years is not spontaneous. It very was hard work!" I said. The doctors are now very supportive, but it was not always like this. Initially I had quite a battle with them, because they wanted to help me and I was refusing their treatments. But now all of the medical teams involved are wonderful and they've been amazed at my results, it's such a great journey.

Now I feel like, no, now I know this is what I'm supposed to be doing with my life. I'm living proof of what life can enable us and empower us to do. If we are prepared to question what is dished out to us in the form of beliefs and conditioning. If we take our own personal connection to our life, we can use that to drive our beliefs and our truth. I'm living proof that you can actually create the life that is going to feed your soul as well as your mouth.

My biggest challenges are in bringing this awareness as a yoga teacher into organisations that consider Yoga to be fluffy, esoteric hippy stuff. Stuff that they think they're not going to benefit from, my wish is to enable them to see how empowering it is at all levels, marrying the ideas of profitable business and the art and science of yoga to grow and expand on all levels. And best of all, it's so much fun! I get to laugh all the time. We cry a lot as well and it's all good.

I can now appreciate a good cry. It's so satisfying to see my own growth and my own evolution, full amazing light bulb moments, you can't beat it. To be able to share that with other people as well just ramps up that lovely feeling.

I'm working with lots of different yoga teachers and groups supporting many different types of clients, the effectiveness of the work that we do is amazing. It can be really simple shifts in your mindset, just to understand that balance between stress and relaxation. That alone really supports people. From a personal satisfaction perspective, that's definitely it.

I've got many new products in the pipeline and am getting more involved in the business world, helping entrepreneurs grow their own businesses but also growing big businesses, which I feel are my own personal roots, that's where I come from; banking, insurance, online gambling. I worked for the government, BUPA, BT, Thomson Holidays - for lots of huge names and because of my vast and varied experiences I know that within huge corporations, it's difficult to look after your staff.

But, I also know, when you do success is guaranteed – the best departments I have ever worked in have had an enlightened manager who is a real leader. One who doesn't interfere with what you do but guides you to the best possible place. To be able to bring that experience to more and more people is very special.

I now train some brilliant yoga teachers and instructors to take the PRIME Profit Paradigm further into the business world, we provide in-house yoga classes, yoga at you desk and workshops and training courses to offer potent and powerful techniques to leadership, management and all teams alike to support everyone within a business to build resilience, improve performance and encourage huge growth and success.

We also run retreats around Europe, Africa and India. The most recent additions to our offerings is the Caribbean, in Mexico and Belize, where we are able to offer an amazing itinerary, the retreat centre is out of this world, food is fresh and nutritious, activities are exciting, fun and will create transformation and development beyond your wildest dreams! These are not just healthy adventure holidays. They are the holiday of a lifetime! Relaxing, replenishing, rejuvenating, rebalancing and transforming.

We also provide amazing adventures for everyone in the family. For business owners who have online business, you can come and if needed do business when you need while the kids get taken on an adventure. The focus will be providing healthy activities, great food and adventure. Offering classes, coaching and courses including yoga, relaxing treatments and other holistic training. Above all having fun and letting your hair down – so local rum and fresh coconuts will definitely be available, or maybe you prefer yours in a pineapple? Taking care of your health it's so important, laughter, adventure, excitement and fun are definitely top of the list. Also great consideration will be given to the food and drinks provided, a carefully considered menu of organic vegetables and fruits provided locally and prepared by expert chiefs will always be available. There will be options of different themes, different events and themes like personal development, or for you perhaps business development and growth, leadership training, or even mind and body detox, healing and we are also formulating a week for internet marketing and business development. There are so many areas where I can offer what I do and I have a great team around me to ensure that this will be an experience that has inevitable evolution.

That's my vision for the opportunities that all businesses and corporates can benefit from – one of my favourite jobs in IT was with Thomson's Holidays. I was there for about four years. It was brilliant. Even though it was a massive business, the fact that you were supplying people with holidays meant that the whole energy of that business had a tinge of holiday magic about it. To create a company that is actually providing holidays for people – being able to offer all the knowledge I've gained through travelling, working and living in so many fascinating and exciting parts of our world, the adventures and wonders, there are so many. I've met the most extraordinary people and visited super interesting places. I'd love to be able to show that to you and at the same time, offer you simple and doable ways of expanding yourself and all levels of who you are and how you live this life.

"Health is the greatest possession.
Contentment is the greatest treasure.
Confidence is the greatest friend.
Non-being is the greatest joy."

- Lao Tzu

Chapter 5

How Yoga Can Help

Physical and mental resilience come as a result of a happier, healthier workforce, supported by collaborative relationships between strong, close knit teams and authentic leaders that respect and align attitudes, beliefs and values, and together take the actions required to go above and beyond – all of this is needed for sustainable expansion and growth into the ever changing technological evolution we are living in.

Are you simply surviving in business like a dinosaur in the industrial age?

Or have you found a way to evolve, expand, thrive and flourish in the digital age?

Has your organisation achieved impressive levels of innovation and workforce efficiency in recent years, and yet, you still require more?

People are stretched so far that they may already feel out of balance. So if the leadership asks even more of them it'll feel like you're trying to "get blood out of a stone", driving the workforce toward their personal vices – there will be more smoking, drinking, blaming and bitching, affairs, gambling, pill popping and all of this is to supposedly deal with the stress and tension.

Build A Resilient Workforce

Stress not only causes pain, stiffness and ill health; it can also bring out all of our obsessions and addictions (and some new ones). Then thinking or feeling out of your box becomes very scary and will be avoided at all costs. Unfortunately this negatively impacts productivity by absorbing energies that usually serve it.

Are you creating new plans for growth? And yet you find that there's no one in place to make it happen?

Fresh new people may be needed to make your plans happen but they must have the help, the support and the connection and buy-in of the existing people. All must be in alignment with the new ideas.

Balance and Alignment

To find balance and alignment you must focus on core competencies, retaining the stable foundation while still being innovative. For this you must pay attention to and support the whole workforce, build resilience and create balance, by understanding all of the following levels: Physical, mental, psychological, social, emotional, financial, environmental, ethical, moral and spiritual.

Having resilience and balance on all levels will ensure holistic health, flexibility, strength and stamina throughout your business. Stress will no longer drain the energies needed to be successful in sustainably and intelligently growing and evolving all areas of business.

Now this may sound like a huge ask, and that is where the art and science of yoga comes into its own. It is a truly holistic system, and the following set of business-focused yoga training systems and educational framework that has been developed to engage all levels of your workforce to achieve all of your desired goals, developing the skills and abilities for holistic resilience, collaborative communication, to unify values, align and expand perspectives across the whole organisation.

Becoming an Authentic Leader

Authentic leaders demonstrate a passion for their purpose, practice their values consistently, and lead with their hearts as well as their heads. They are open, honest and full of integrity, establishing long-term meaningful relationships and have the self-discipline (*Tapas*) to get results. They know who they are *(Swadyaya)*.

> *"Let the Beauty we love, be what we do."*
> -Rumi

I don't believe there is a standard set of "authenticity characteristics" that leaders are born with, but I do believe we are all capable of emerging from our own life experiences as authentic leaders. By consistently testing ourselves consciously and subconsciously as we go through our life experiences, learning from so-called mistakes or potentially harmful or damaging situations we encounter as we go through life, reframing our story to understand who we are at the deepest core of our being. In doing so we can discover the purpose of our leadership and learn that by being truly ourselves, by being authentic we automatically become more effective.

I encourage you to do this so that you can discover your potential right now. The challenge is to understand yourself well enough to discover where you can use your leadership gifts to serve others.

Discovering your authentic leadership requires commitment to developing yourself, devoting yourself to a lifetime of realising your potential. Take responsibility, developing yourself.

Frame (or reframe) your life story in ways that allow you to see that you are not a passive observer of life but you are an individual who can cultivate self-awareness to enable you to evolve and grow from your experiences.

With that awareness you can then practice your own values and principles, even if it puts you at risk, be careful to balance your motivations so you are driven by these inner values as much as by desire for external rewards or recognition.

Keep a strong support team around you who will ensure that you live an integrated and grounded life.

Yamas and *Niyamas,* the first to steps of the eight in Patanjali's *Astanga* are the ground work and will culminate in you becoming your own authentic self. Don't harm or be greedy, be honest and realistic, use your energies wisely, work hard at what is truly important to you, know yourself and be humble with natural forces greater than you.

If you are both psychologically self-aware and philosophically ethically sound, then leadership becomes an emergent quality from within. Being a role model not a dictator, characterised by trust and integrity because you possess a high level of self-awareness, then naturally outcomes, such as optimism, trust and the quality of relationships are more influential and the resulting positive impact is increased.

Consider the following Yoga definitions:

"To unite and come together"

"To tie the strands of the mind together"

"To attain what was previously unattainable"

Yoga as an art and a science provides the philosophy and theory, the tools and the methods needed to support the aims and objectives of your company. The science is founded in the experience of dedicated and diligent sages over millennia of practise and study. The art is the application of the knowledge that efficiently and effectively achieves the desired goal.

So what is this system?

The PRIME Profit Paradigm™

To stay competitive and continue to grow, CEOs and leadership teams must strive to find breakthrough, leading edge performance and productivity gains from employees in the current rapidly changing landscape.

The PRIME Profit Paradigm™ focuses on five key areas needed to ensure expansion of all areas and a true evolution of your business.

This Unique Training System – is the only comprehensive and business focused yoga training available today. Specifically targeted to create growth in your organisation and shift it into the new paradigm – The Digital Age. We look individually at each of the five key areas indicated by PRIME to take you forward into the new paradigm.

P – People

R – Relationships

I – Innovation

M – Mindset

E – Evolution

Each of the following systems is a workshop in its own right as well as a component of the holistic and integrated solution. There are many more resources available on the website that supports this book, use the access code "Pancha Kosha"

Click to Register HERE for Exclusive Updates!

www.corporateyogalondon.com

Growing Your Business

Lord Young released his 'Growing Your Business' report in May 2013. In it he has highlight three areas that he believes create the right conditions for businesses to fulfil their growth potential.

The message is that for businesses to thrive and grow they are looking for three things:

The Three C's of Business Growth!

1. Confidence – not only in the economy and overall prospects for growth, but also in their conviction to make it happen

2. Capability – by improving a firm's health, resilience, skills and performance

3. Coherence – businesses need support that is designed and marketed in a way that everybody

involved including the customers, can understand, can trust and can find.

The PRIME profit paradigm™ has all of these components inherent within its truly holistic and integrated design:

P=People with Capability

R=Relationships with Coherence

I=Innovation with Confidence

M=Mindset with Courage and Conviction

E=Evolution, Expansion and Growth

Creating Intelligent, Sustainable Growth.

Evolving your business with intelligent and sustainable expansion requires a big leap, a leap that maybe into the unknown.

To grow and operate at a size that you have never been before is after all unknown.

A new perspective is needed.

When you find that new perspective you have entered a New Paradigm.

The New Paradigm

That is the purpose of this book, and this detailed and modulated programme of training is to support you and guide you through this change, assist you in creating real change, a transformative experience that will bring you to this unknown territory, into the new paradigm.

You can try the "drip... drip... drip" approach. Things may change eventually. But will it be the change you wanted? Will it be substantial enough, and in the required time?

With each drip you carry a lot of past with you so you really can't change into something new, you may achieve a rehashed version of what was...

Is that what you want?

Real transformation to a place of true growth and an ability to sustain growth is where this book and the training we offer will take you. It's like a butterfly, a transmutation of the organism like a caterpillar shifting to the next stage: the cocoon.

And inside the cocoon it's chaos. Pure chaos. If this stage is seen in isolation it appears like total madness. But when you take a step back and look at the bigger picture then you understand this chaos is a part of the process required for the transformation from creepy crawly leaf-eating machine into amazing flying, nectar drinking, egg producing and oh so beautiful butterfly. Stepping back allows us to witness the chaos in-between the two stages of stability.

You must remember that this chaos is to be expected and has to be truly embraced. The PRIME Profit Paradigm facilitates the opening up, the shifting of perspective required to do this.

Transformation Through Chaos

To be prepared for chaos and to come out of it sane and transformed needs resilience. Maintaining momentum, so you don't suddenly pull back into conflicts of the past.

Allowing and accepting the chaos, embracing it as a necessary step to then move forward with sufficient momentum, ensures that you definitely reach the new transformed organism or organisation.

Maintaining momentum has to happen within the culture. Through all levels of the culture, and as with the butterfly there are three parts:

1. Growth of people as individuals and as a team.

2. Growth in leadership – in the systems and processes, the processes that are done by the individual. You are also growing from that.

3. Growth of the business and because you grow the business, you grow the profits. So everybody gets to contribute to, evolve and grow from the experience.

Because of the rapid pace of change that exists and everything appears to move so quickly, so chaotically in today's markets, it can feel like everything is totally out of balance.

You want your people to work hard, but they are naturally fearful and worried about moving into chaos; they want to stay comfortable, but that means staying in the past, that kind of comfort is stagnant. It's the caterpillar.

Because you are trying to get more and more from the people, from the teams, from yourself, everyone becomes so stressed and worried about moving into the chaos, they stuff the stress down, behaving in ways that enables them to forget about their worries, in come all their vices (and yours too). All the things that fear, stress and tension bring and make us do.

When people feel this level of stress they feel isolated, separate and this will often result in bitching, backbiting, addictive behaviours, loose canons, trying to deflect problems; hiding from their feelings. That's what we do, it's even socially accepted, because people don't want to be in the chaos and are filled with fear.

Mistakes – Are You Out of Your Box?

How can you encourage the workforce and yourself to be happy to feel out of your comfort zone? After all that's where the chaos is. And maybe fresh new people need to be brought in to help and support the process, which is fine as long as they can connect and engage with the people that you already have and everybody is prepared to step into the chaos together, supporting each other and moving forward into this new future.

Using a variety of yoga techniques and developing new skills and perspectives is how an organisation can thrive, a workforce that is immune to the paralysing complexities of change, willing to collaborate with a wider range of individuals is absolutely necessary today.

Staff with a stronger aptitude in the new core skills is essential – BUT - there is no substitute for experience. The competencies essential to strong performance are best developed through on-the-job experience with a single company over time, treating your workforce with respect and honour, offering them opportunities to grow and flourish as individuals will increase the likelihood of retaining then.

109

The existing people must be re-aligned with the new ideas and be able to find the harmony and balance, focusing on their core competencies, on what they are already good at and assisting them to develop further so that they feel supported enough to explore who they are and who they can become and at the same time find ways to manage stress and release fear.

Once you understand how to release the fear, you are then able to create an uninhibited environment, a creative and innovative environment. One in which mistakes are allowed, even encouraged, because it is through mistakes that the biggest best learning happens. When people are allowed to freely explore without fear then it is possible to make great successes, they are allowed to be and recognised for feeling outside their comfort zone. You acknowledge that that's a really great thing for them to do.

For all this you need something that is called equanimity. It's calm, serene, balanced, and you need equanimity in all areas. Taking a leap of faith and finding this intimate space where the chaos is, is what yoga, through its many practises, really helps to bring to the forefront.

One of the definitions of yoga is to unite. Another way of defining yoga is to attain what was previously unattainable. That's how your business can really benefit from the wisdom yoga offers.

The PRIME Profit Paradigm - The perfect way to get you, your people and teams, and your business on track for huge growth and success.

Pancha Kosha

The five bodies or five layers, like the Russian dolls, Matryoshka, that fit one inside another, is the key to this success.

People Relating Innovatively with Mindsets aligned will Evolve!

AnnaMayaKosha – The People

The first layer is called 'food' and it's the physical layer.

PranaMayaKosha – The Relationships

The second layer is called *Prana*, which is the energy, the relationships, how things interact and communicate with each other.

ManoMayaKosha – The Innovation

The third layer is the mental body. Mano is understood as one reason that we as Man are different from animals. At this level we begin to link into the mental faculties we have as humans, why we have been able to develop technologies (like computers) and why dogs or monkeys can't.

VijnanaMayaKosha – The Mindset

The fourth layer is higher intelligence or wisdom. We receive information and we can process it and that's what makes us men. But what is it that makes us genius? This is where we look at the *vijnanamayakosha*. It's that genius, that ability to see something that is completely out of the ordinary, out of the box. Like a child, like Einstein.

111

The final Kosha is *Ananda* this means 'bliss'. This kosha is expansive, ecstatic, the connection back to the core consciousness or universal consciousness. Some people call it God, some people call it the matrix, the field or even universal consciousness. We have so many different names for it and it's represented in different ways.

From the *Pancha kosha* we have the framework for the complete system that is –

The P.R.I.M.E. Profit Paradigm™

P – People - AnnaMayaKosha

R – Relationships - PranaMayaKosha

I – Innovation - ManoMayaKosha

M – Mindset - VijnanaMayaKosha

E – Evolution - AnandaMayaKosha

Pancha Kosha – The Five Layers of Existence.

The aim of yoga is to attain higher levels of consciousness by penetrating one kosha after the other with our awareness. All yogic practices facilitate this. There are physical practices of hatha yoga like *asanas,* postures and *kriyas,* internal cleansing techniques to clear, purify and open the layer of the body, the *annamayakosha.* This frees, balances and harmonises the flow of energy known as *prana*, as you advance in your physical practice the range of influence becomes subtler and the energy is more directly influenced.

113

The physical practices are also used as preparation for breathing practices called *pranayama*. As they purify the body from toxins and assist in further influencing the pranamayakosha and indirectly affecting the subtler *manomayakosha*. When the first two layers are cleansed and purified, meditation practices of raja yoga become easier and begin to open up perception and innovation. At this stage, there is no longer any barrier between the body and the mind. Energy becomes aligned so the body and mind and can work in unison. Clarity comes intuitively and effortlessly so the evolution to higher state of consciousness emerges naturally.

"Burdens are the foundations of ease and bitter things the forerunners of pleasure."

-Rumi

People

People in any business, in fact in any situation, relate to each other as the individuals – we are all individuals relating – That's life! And whether that be to colleagues, to leadership, to suppliers, to clients and customers, it can also be to processes and procedures, it is here where innovation enables, generates and allows for real expansion resulting in subsequent evolution.

When everything is in alignment, from *annamayakosha* to *anandamayakosha* the whole organism expands, the individual expands, the leadership expands – everyone grows, evolves and benefits.

> *"You don't build a business,*
> *you build people*
> *and then people build the business"*
>
> -Zig Ziglar

The individual parts of a business are the people, and for any business to thrive and evolve every individual part must be resilient, physically and mentally. Here are the four key elements for personal resilience:

> 1 = Health & fitness
>
> 2 = Flexibility & suppleness
>
> 3 = Strength & power
>
> 4 = Endurance & stamina

To help you to build resilience into the workforce, we have two training systems. Using theses we have devised an approach that leads to a realisation of the self-healing powers of your body and then recognition of the immense growth potential that bringing real sustainable transformation and evolution to a more powerful, robust, organism – profitable, expanding, exciting and fun organisation and unsurpassed work/life balance.

System1 – Physical Progressor ™

The Physical Progressor™ Is a complete lifestyle template that we build together. Using the three key skills of awareness, understanding and (new) action to begin the process of building physical and mental resilience. This system is based around the *Yogachara* model and it's four key concepts: *Ahara, Vihara, Achara* and *Vichara*.

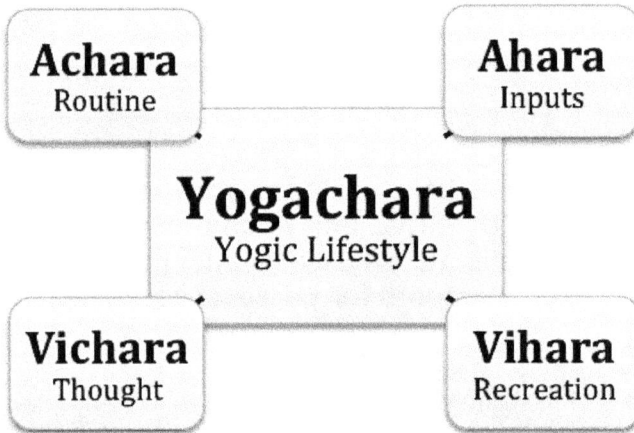

Achara
Routine

Ahara
Inputs

Yogachara
Yogic Lifestyle

Vichara
Thought

Vihara
Recreation

In the face of pain, stiffness, fever, asthma, cold, cancer, gout, arthritis, high blood pressure, addictions, infidelity, mood swings, depression, panic, anxiety, stagnant, fear … or whatever holds you back, these are all attributable to an imbalance in one or more of the four recommended parameters of a holistic and integrated yogic lifestyle.

Ahara

Inputs. This refers to all that you receive. Thoughts, information, traditions, food, drink, music, culture, even the chemicals you use to clean your house, whatever you bring in. Using discernment and discrimination *Viveka,* it's possible to cleanse and purify all inputs and the result is a clean and pure body.

Ahara refers to having a balanced diet of all inputs, including food, physical products and information, ideas, teachings, extending even to the company you keep. All physical and sensory inputs.

Vichara

Positive thinking. Through practicing a variety of meditative practices, guided meditations and visualisation, you gradually become increasingly aware of your thoughts. You will begin to notice things, becoming more aware of yourself and your patterns of thoughts, feeling and behaviours. Over time you can develop this awareness and you'll notice when you feel uncomfortable and as your awareness grows you'll come to know that for every uncomfortable feeling there is an associated thought. As soon as you notice it feels uncomfortable, you'll be able to say, "Okay, what is the negative thought here?" become aware of that thought can then begin the journey of understanding what's needed to really look at the thought which will automatically lead to the negative aspect dissolving this understanding means converting old negatives into new and positive wisdom, learning

117

and so there is a natural switching into a positive thought.

This concept of *vihara* helps to manage thoughts, opinions, behaviours and attitudes, encouraging you to spend time generating, developing and deepening positivity. Maintaining healthy thoughts requires awareness, discipline, duty and faith, to cultivate them we use the *Parikarmas,* embellishments to beautify the mind.

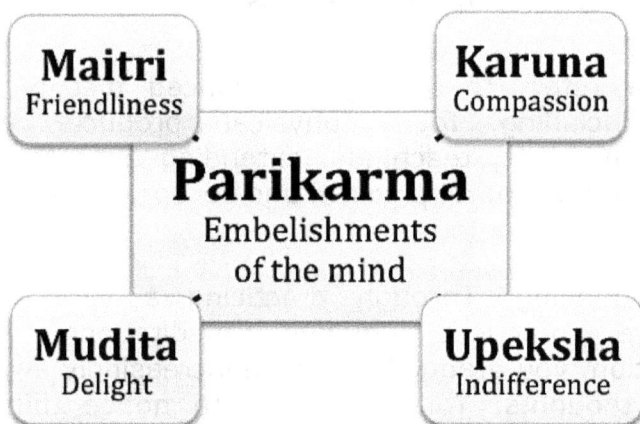

Maitri
Friendliness

Karuna
Compassion

Parikarma
Embelishments
of the mind

Mudita
Delight

Upeksha
Indifference

1. Maitri – friendliness toward others regardless of how they behave.

2. Karuna – compassion (action in empathy)

3. Mudita – joy in others joy and in the virtuous, able to laugh at yourself

4. Upeksha – benevolent indifference – compassionate detachment and disregard to the vices of others (and self) gentle, graceful, non

judgemental, allowing and accepting, learning and growing. This one is so tricky!

"Pleasure is always derived from something outside you, whereas joy arises from within."
— Eckhart Tolle

The more you practice these *parikarmas*, the more they happen automatically and eventually you'll realise you started feeling badly and without even trying, you flipped back into feeling good. So you go from negative to positive without any effort at all and in no time at all.

Achara

Feeling good. In order to feel good, there are two things that you want to develop. The first one is to create routines, and using the natural cycles that exist in all part of nature, external and internal, arriving at a place of balance and harmony, where energies are maximised and all of the bodies systems are enhanced and optimised, this is *Achara*. Having routines that follow natural cycles, like sleeping, eating, exercising, working, enhance the natural regulation of the body, this feels really good. Discipline becomes an automatic result of sticking to routine – and when I use the word discipline I mean anything that we do regularly and frequently.

This concept *Achara* also results in a more streamlined character, good conduct, giving up negative habits, choosing to live by good values.

The underlying construct of *Achara,* with it's routines and conduct will support and enhance time management and planning – developing the sound routines that will give you freedom.

Vihara

Relaxation and recreation. There is another way to consider this word re-creation it has an aspect that represents the re creation of our energies or ourselves, through rest and play. This concept can be even further broken down in the following areas:

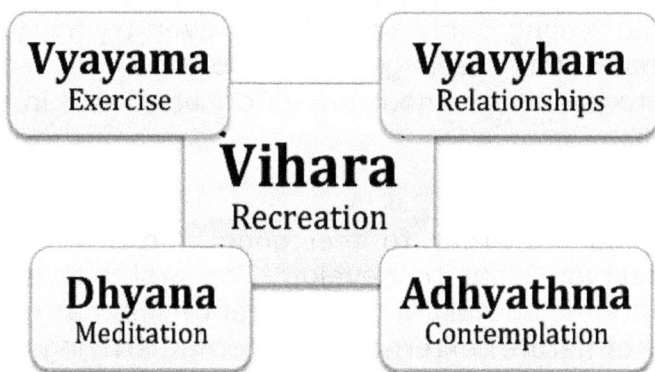

Vyayama
Exercise

Vyavyhara
Relationships

Vihara
Recreation

Dhyana
Meditation

Adhyathma
Contemplation

I.   Vyayam - regularly exercising
II. Vyavahar - maintaining healthy inter-personal relationships
III. Dhyan – meditating to maintaining inner silence and peace
IV. Adhyathma - contemplating life with a holistic spiritual outlook

Transformation requires an immense amount of energy, to facilitate transformation and evolution *Vihara* is vital. When a caterpillar transforms into a butterfly, it passes through its own period of re-creation. It re-creates itself when it sits inside its cocoon and chaos is going on within the cocoon, but

120

for all intents and purposes, it's appears from the outside as if it's dead.

In the same way, we can view the way the body can facilitate its own recovery, sometimes people go into a coma in order to allow the body time and energy to heal, and then they may come out completely recovered. There is a type of re-creation going on.

How can you re-create yourself? What do you do to relax? What methods and processes do you use that are recreational tools?

"Leave all the afternoon for exercise and recreation, which are as necessary as reading. I will rather say more necessary because health is worth more than learning".
-Thomas Jefferson

Consider the word 'recreation' or the phrase 'recreational activities'; these refer to finding ways to enjoy yourself and re-create yourself which will bring about a sense of relaxation and nurturing.

You can re-create in lots of different ways. You pull that phrase apart and think about the re-creational aspect of it, from here think about *Ahara*, what is it you are putting in? What thoughts do you use to help you maintain that recreation? Then consider *Vihara* and you can come up the aspect *Achara,* and with a very positive healthy living lifestyle – and that is *yogachara* and it will facilitate our Physical Progression.

121

System 2 – Productive Perception Processor™

In order to ensure that all teaching and training provided is accessible to and serving each individual within the workforce we now consider each individual.

Learning styles are as individual as people, but they are always composed of the five basic methods of sensory perception that bring the information into the mind: V.A.K.O.G - (Visual, Auditory, Kinaesthetic, Olfactory and Gustatory)

Then the next stage of the process is how we cognise (our cognitive processing) where the information brought in is processed and becomes knowledge, which in turn leads to both an ability to communicate and share as well as the necessary motor function needed to do the skill or action.

We all learn in different ways, and on different days each individual may also learn in different ways. There are four distinct learning styles, and there is a cycle through which we pass, with four key stages in order to learn a new skill.

"Knowledge is power, and the right knowledge lets man perform miraculous, almost godlike tasks."
— Dan Brown,

The Productive Perception Processor™ - also works with the three different types of *Pramana* right knowledge, which according to Patanjali are:

1. *Pratyaksha* - direct perception or cognition

2. *Anumana* - inference, reasoning, deduction

3. *Agamah* - authority, testimony, validation, competent evidence

When you understand how you learn best, what your personal preferences are, then you can ensure that those methods are always available to you during any training, that way ensuring that all lessons actually stick, staying in your mind, so that you can then either go on and teach someone else what you are learning, or you can use what you are learning in a way that really works for you.

The model we use is fluid and elegant, offering both a way to understand individual people's different learning styles, and an explanation of a cycle of experiential learning that applies to us all.

Many brilliant and successful executives and strategists recognise the value of knowledge as a primary driving source for a company's sustainable competitive advantage, there is even a position in some companies, called the chief knowledge officer (CKO). However, many people have proposed differing perspectives and models relating to the concept of knowledge management. In The Productive Perception Processor™ we examine differing knowledge management viewpoints, by examining and integrating those viewpoints and theories and subsequently relating them to the yogic concepts of perception, how it is and how it can be managed and shifted through training and techniques available in the vast yoga tool kit.

The roles of change agents, innovators, and opinion leaders, such as CKOs, are explored in terms of effective knowledge management strategies and techniques. A model and strategies are proposed that can serve as a framework for your knowledge management change agents to effectively facilitate the acquisition and use of knowledge in your company by effectively using an organisational memory system and cyclical learning model with a central principle that experiential learning is the key.

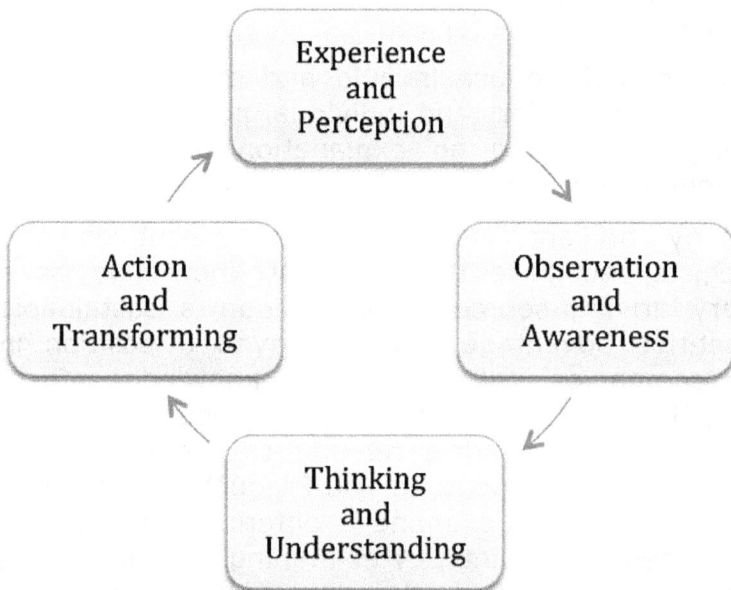

Experience and Perception

Observation and Awareness

Thinking and Understanding

Action and Transforming

There are four stages in the cycle of learning, in which concrete experiences provide a basis for observations and reflections. These observations and reflections are assimilated and gathered into abstract concepts producing new implications for action which can be actively tested in turn creating new experiences.

This process represents a learning cycle where the person learning experiences, reflects, thinks and acts so they can actively test and experiment with, which in turn enable the creation of new skills and experiences.

And then once you have learnt how to do it, you go back around the cycle to the feeling place and say: 'Am I doing it right? Do I need to go around it again?'

Relationships

In this section we look at communication and relationships from every dimension.

In relationships you connect and there can be transference of information, you may have information, knowledge or wisdom that you want to communicate to the other, or there is something outside of yourself that has information that you want to take in.

You don't speak because you want to simply make noise; you speak because you want somebody to hear and understand what you are saying, and to get your message across.

In the same way, you don't have a cup because it looks nice. You have a cup because it's good at holding tea and you want to drink from it. It's all about the purpose of something. I know there are some of you reading this who are very fussy about your cups, but for the sake of the metaphor stay with me!

You must connect in order to communicate (transmit or receive) that information and this connection is the relationship.

Whether that be connecting people to the bigger picture so they become aware of the process from a higher or a different perspective, or communicating the specific details of the individual tasks that they are responsible for – the ability to connect is a key skill for all great leaders – make em wanna folla!!

Another important consideration in relationships is the fact that we have one mouth and two ears, the wise amongst us know we should use them in proportion and listen at least twice as much as we speak!

Not understanding or appreciating what is being communicated will result in pain: shame, blame, disagreement, rivalry, dislike, gangs, separation, arguments, confusion, competition, conflict, wasting time, and reduced productivity – starving the energy out of your company.

This multi dimensional approach to communicating and relating can be very clearly understood by using a model based on the seven chakras. The chakras are from an ancient tantric way of looking at the energy body. The main difference between tantric yoga and hatha yoga is that hatha yoga looks at the dualities, the polarities, the good and the bad. Tantric is the good and bad – two sides of the same coin. *Tantra* is the coin, hatha yoga is the two sides.

So, when we are looking at *tantra* yoga, we are looking at the relationship between two things, where the two polarities come together.

"The most damaging phrase in the language is: 'It's always been done that way.'"

- Grace Hopper

A group of scientists interested in behaviour and social responses and conditioning devised an experiment where they placed five monkeys in a cage and in the middle, a ladder with fresh, ripe bananas on the top.

Every time a monkey went up the ladder, the scientists soaked the rest of the monkeys with cold water, they hated this. So whenever a monkey went up the ladder, the others beat it up.

After some time, no monkey dared to go up the ladder regardless of the temptation.

Then one of the monkeys was replaced. As soon as this new monkey saw the ripe bananas, it did what any (unconditioned) red-blooded money would! It went up the ladder. Immediately the other monkeys beat it up. By now no water was required.

After several beatings, the new member learned not to climb the ladder even though it never knew why (conditioned).

A second monkey was substituted and the same occurred. The first monkey participated in the beating. A third monkey was changed and the same was repeated (beating). The fourth was substituted and the beating was repeated and finally the fifth monkey was replaced.

What was left was a group of five monkeys, none of whom had ever received the cold shower, and none of whom would have attempted to climb the ladder.

This story can go some way to helping understand why we continue to do what we are doing if there is a different way out there that serves us better then change is great.

System 3 – The 7 C's Of Relating™

The root chakra: Community

The root chakra, or base chakra is the lowest in the body, connecting us to our community, to our tribe.

Here we can consider our connection to traditions, conditioning, superstitions; unconscious and inherited belief patterns and social structures. These are often at play as we relate to the tribe that sustains us. From

128

this context we must consider that we so often operate at an unconscious, conditioned, conditional and survival level. It's a very low level, and can even be a superficial level.

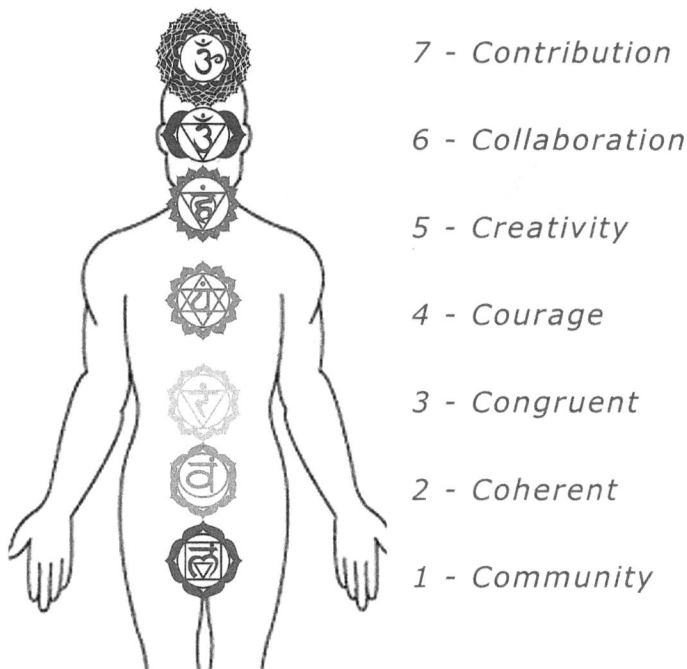

7 - *Contribution*

6 - *Collaboration*

5 - *Creativity*

4 - *Courage*

3 - *Congruent*

2 - *Coherent*

1 - *Community*

The sacral chakra: Coherent

Coherent content. Can we connect to the communication shared through the relationship emotionally? Is it coherent to us? Does it make sense to us? It's the content and context of that which we are communicating actually saying what we want it to, not just saying something from a temporary emotional state, a consistent connection allowing the message to be communicated effectively to all involved.

The solar plexus chakra: Congruent

The next level is personal power. Is it for me? Does it fit me? Is it congruent so that it is right for me now? Whatever my goal is, whatever my purpose, my aims, my values are... Is this communication congruent, meaning is it aligned so that there is no disturbance or conflict with my beliefs and values and does it have integrity to me and where I am at right now?

The heart chakra: Courageous

Then comes is the heart, from here we want the communication to be courageous, can we be open hearted and speak from our hearts? This is now about wanting the communication to be heart felt, authentic and perhaps even vulnerable, there is much more feeling, a love-based alignment, like spiritually we are aligned here.

The throat chakra: Creativity

The next is the throat chakra, where we look at communication being clear and to do so we can use our creativity, we have different learning styles. This means we have to learn to speak creatively. To facilitate all of those different styles in understanding what we mean by what we say and how we communicate it.

Some people learn through touch, others through experience, others by a mixture of styles. To reach everyone, teaching and speaking styles must incorporate everything, such as role-playing, story telling, activities and metaphors.

The third eye chakra: Collaboration

The third eye relates to concepts relating to intuition and extra sensory perception; you are able to pick up on so many signals verbal and nonverbal. Let's look at body language, when you realise that most people are not consciously aware of the subtle (and not so subtle) signals they are constantly giving out. You may think words are important, but seventy per cent of how you understand somebody is through body language and is non-verbal. So through the third eye, you can understand how to make a more profound connection. There has to be a deep, fundamental connection outside of the spoken word.

The communication here is through real connection and collaboration. Each individual component in the workforce, each individual person, is as valuable as the next. With that realised, there is real collaboration. It doesn't matter how many mistakes you make, there are going to be a number of areas at which you personally excel and others will look to you and respect you. When there is this respect within the team, everyone feels like they are pulling together and recognised as equally valuable regardless of the role they play within the team. That's what collaboration is all about.

The crown Chakra: Contribution

The final chakra is the crown chakra on top of the head, which is about contributions, about being able to manifest something that contributes to the greater good of the individual, the team and the whole organisation.

> *"To listen well is as powerful a*
> *means of communication and*
> *influence as to talk well"*
> *- John Marshall*

Innovation

If you want to be a pioneer, on the leading edge then you must to be able to also inspire the rest of the workforce to encourage them, facilitate them in also being creative and allowing innovation without any fear. Innovation is really about leadership, about the processes and principles.

When you take personal responsibility for your job and for your actions, take ownership and have authenticity, autonomy and accountability, then you don't need to rely upon authoritative managers, they can sometimes cause confusion, especially if they want to retain too much control and insist on too many rules and regulations – that stifle creativity.

"Outstanding leaders go out of their way to boost the self esteem of their personnel. If people believe in themselves it s amazing what they can accomplish."

\- Sam Walton

You can't do without management, but the more closely aligned they are with the workforce, and the more like leaders they are, the more they just seem to fit in. They are fundamentally information workers and in that role they are crucial. Especially today, because we have so much data that we can collect and manipulate and extrapolate so much information – there are gazillions of terabytes available to us and using the right data and the right processes to make the right choices and decisions can result in us thriving or dying as a business. Managers must be perceptive, open minded and flexible and more.

System 4 – The Influential Innovator™

In yoga, there are 3 basic principles of nature called the Gunas. There is constant movement and friction between these principles and as such they create the stuff of life from the potential and non-manifest to the manifest.

For the basic understanding of these principles let's look at the simplified concepts of the three Gunas. One is *Tamas*, which is about physical matter. Two is *Rajas*, which is about energy and heat that transforms physical matter. The third is *Sattva*, which is balanced and harmonious, it represents the purity of the natural world when *rajas* and *tamas* are in balance.

By identifying how these three principles can be applied to different aspects of yourself or of your business it is possible to use the profound wisdom within their concepts to bring many components into balance.

Tamas: The People – developing and sustaining physical and mental resilience.

Rajas: The Leaders – developing inspiring, innovative and authentic strategists and managers.

Sattva: The Organisation – delivering successful growth, dynamic and leading edge processes, expanding top line revenues and bottom line profits.

Tamas – Physical matter

133

You need *Tamas* because you need physical material, but on its own its deadly; it's heavy and it doesn't go anywhere, and it can use and absorb a lot of energy and resources.

Rajas – Movement

You need *Rajas* to get the energy going, but if you go too far, things end up on fire. A result of too much *rajas*, that's out of balance.

Sattva – Balance

If you get it right, the balance between the two becomes *Sattvic*: Pure, harmonious and balanced.

Again the stunning Lotus flower makes an appearance! The amazing lotus flower growing in muddy water. It needs Tamas to sprout the seeds and to feed the roots through the soil. Then it needs the stem that grows through the water to help to support the flower on the top and the flower is the balance and beauty of the whole thing. A pristine, clean, waterproof, bright flower emerges from the mucky soil and dirty waters to bloom in all its *sattvic* glory.

When you look at those processes in order. At the bottom you have inertia (*tamas*) darkness, heaviness, and material.

Then we move up to *rajas*, and that's change, action, energy, raw creativity and movement.

Then once you reach *sattva*, there's harmony, beingness, purity, ripe, balance and light.

Observing and learning from how these three work together, we can really get a grip on how leadership and processes in leadership are going to help generate equanimity of balance.

When you are looking at the way a business works, you want to use all the people in the business. You want to communicate and have them communicating with each other through all the levels, because we are willing to be inspired, we are all prepared to be innovative so that we can lead and be led to a goal that is going to benefit everybody.

System 5 – Three Killer KPIs™

To manage processes and operations there are key performance indicators (KPIs), a very popular business term. People in business are always asking 'How are your KPIs?' – in the PRIME Profit Paradigm™ you have a powerful way to ensure success:

- Knowledge
- Practice
- Intelligence

Are you performing in a way that is going to get you to your goal?

What indicators can you draw up and measure to ensure that you are on track? If you're not performing appropriately, how do you steer yourself back to the right track?

An aeroplane spends ninety-nine per cent of its time off track, it is the pilots job to continuously adjust to and follow the non-linear route, as this what they always take, to avoid air traffic, weather systems and the like, and so the pilot continuously must steer the plane back on track. In business you have to maintain the lowest cost that you can, maintaining the quality expected, and at the same time generating the highest profit you can.

From a personal perspective you want the same. By asking yourself "How can I reach my personal goals without giving up all of my energies to get there?"

The three killer KPI's program helps you identify exactly how to drive yourself, your workforce and your business to achieve killer performance, productivity and profits.

Key person of influence... Using knowledge to identify that person (or system) be it yourself or the leader or the CEO or the person sitting next to you – who is it that influences best you when you are doing your job.

Key practice of inspiration... what is it in the company or who is it in the company that inspires you? Where do you find the wisdom, the insights and the support to take you to take the right steps and practice the right actions to take you to your goal?

Killer performance Innovator. Who is the killer performer around you that can utilise intelligence and will absolutely get the job done, in the optimum time and to the highest quality? The one you can model, who is a key influencer and inspiration for the rest of the team? Offering insightful wisdom and optimum performance? The killer performance innovator will always have loads of imagination, the right intention, and so reach the right goals in the best way possible. They will be able to encourage others, and so will positively impact every aspect of the business.

All managers and leaders must fit this frame or they need to know who is the go-to person for the best person or resource in your company for the specific task in hand.

How do you identify and build new skills?

Who are the high-performing employees in todays work environment?

What skills and behaviours differentiate your most productive employees?

"The difference between a positive spirit and a positive attitude is that one comes from the heart and the other from the head."

-Amanda Gore

Most managers and performance management models assume that strong business acumen, task and process mastery, and technical know-how are the key requirements for the majority of an employee's job performance. Unfortunately, the prevalence of these now out-dated assumptions about the most valuable skills and abilities means you cannot clearly identify your organisation's next generation of high performers with this mindset, these are the dinosaurs. The majority of organisations use out dated methods, and are likely to fail to identify 65% of their new high performers. Those who do are going to thrive in this digital age, this new paradigm.

Identifying new high performers to build the next generation of employees requires focusing on the ten core employee competencies that differentiate the people who are best able to perform in the new work environment:

1. Prioritisation
2. Teamwork
3. Organisational awareness
4. Problem solving
5. Self-awareness
6. Proactivity
7. Influence
8. Decision making
9. Learning agility
10. Technical expertise

Based on these differentiating core competencies, the new high performer is someone who can:

Adapt to Change: Using their knowledge of the organisation and their role to quickly adjust to work environment changes. They are adaptive, proactive, not paralyzed by change, and they are willing to take action that move projects and priorities forward.

Work Collaboratively: Good collaborators work well with and through others. They have the teamwork skills necessary to work with a wide range of people across your organisation. They use their own technical expertise or the technical expert they know will influence stakeholders and contribute effectively to collaborative projects.

Apply Judgment: Using strong analytic skills to prioritise their work, assess problems, and make decisions. They rely on their expertise, experience, and knowledge of the organisation to apply judgment to their decisions and in their work.

Knowledge, information, and wisdom.

With the arrival of the information age, the digital revolution, there's a huge amount of knowledge available to everybody. It's like having all of the knowledge from the whole world available and at your fingertips and then there's the interconnectedness between people, so many people. Now while it's great to have all of that accessible to you, there is also a danger of drowning in knowledge and information, death by information overload! By drowning I mean that the mind gets bombarded with this huge excess of input, that you miss something that is essential for your goals or your purpose. As a human life, with a purpose, in order to be truly fulfilled – you must find that place of peace, inner peace, of stillness; it's a place that is described by many masters as "the source of all intelligence" and it is here where innovation exists, where wisdom resides.

So many people don't even realise it exists within them.

My understanding of innovation and the core of what spirituality means is just that. By spirituality I don't mean having a particular belief structure, or subscribing to a particular doctrine or set of thoughts. Spirituality is for me has been discovering a dimension within myself that transcends the continuous movement of thoughts of thinking, the dimension where wisdom resides.

139

Mindset

Mindset is about thoughts, beliefs, attitudes and values. When everyone contributing within one organisation is going to create the best possible outcome for everyone's highest good, then you have the perfect mindset alignment. In order to get this alignment, you have to look at people's individual needs, beliefs and attitudes, and how all of these drive their behaviour, after all it is behaviour or action that gets the job done. Behaviour is your bottom line. In order to influence behaviour, you have to look at the values, the beliefs and attitudes that incorporate the human needs.

By encouraging people to be clear about their objectives and then defining clear strategies to achieve them aligns attitudes, beliefs, thoughts and actions. Clarity of understanding is needed to achieve your potential in any area of life or work.

System 6 – Mindset Mastery™

Vyasa, who wrote a commentary on the yoga sutras, helps us have a more expanded perspective and clearer, deeper understanding of the meaning of these valuable sutras. Vyasa defined five states of *citta* (mind): restless (*ksipta*), listless (*mudha*), distracted (*viksipta*) focused (*ekagra*) and controlled (*niruddha*)

This model helps understand the mind by identifying its varied states and activities according to the mind's development and spiritual refinement. This model can also be used to describe a company's preparedness for inspired innovative practice and evolution.

State	Guna	Symptom	Cause	Inclination	Vritti
Mudha Dull	Tamas (inertia)	Sleep, delusion, fear, laziness	Lust, anger, greed, infatuation	Vice	Outgoing and all sided
Ksipta Distracted	Rajas (activity)	Pain, worry, fickle, selfish actions	Attachment, hatred, selfishness	Virtue, vice	Outgoing and all sided
Viksipta Concentrated	Mixed Sattwa	Joy, patience, virtuous qualities, selfless actions	Selflessness, righteousness	Knowledge, virtue, dispassion, spiritual prosperity	Ingoing and beginning of Samadhi
Ekagrata One-pointed	Pure Sattwa	Increasing detachment	Lower dispassion	Wisdom	One-pointed Lower Samadhi
Niroddha Controlled	Involution of the gunas	Abiding in the Self	Supreme dispassion	Kaivalya Liberation	Controlled Higher Samadhi

This classification may be helpful for you as a manager or maybe a business owner who needs to assess your company, workforce or any individual employees' readiness for change and growth, and then find the appropriate tools, techniques and practices to ensure expansion and evolution. It can also be helpful for you as an individual who needs to measure your own progress.

We all experience each of these states at different times, tending to flit around and among them. What enables you to spend more of your life in the more desirable states of mind is the entire practice of yoga, as defined by Patanjalis' eight steps – *astanga*, including ethical conduct, *asana*, *pranayama*, and meditation.

KSIPTA - This is this lowest state of mind. You will be highly agitated and unable to think, listen or keep quiet. "It's like a monkey jumping up and down," T.K.V. Desikachar says. "Toss it a diamond, and it doesn't know what it is."

This first stage is the stage in which the mind is flung about, often called "Monkey Mind", and it is representative of the early stage of humanity, or, in man, the mind of the child. It is restless, wandering and continually distracted. Darting constantly from one object to another, distracted by every shinny bright thing, it corresponds to activity on the physical plane.

Ksipta is the natural state of the mind that hasn't yet been trained. The mind has by nature the tendency to go outward and lose itself in sense impressions, desires and worries.

MUDHA - In this state, no information seems to reach the brain. The mind is dull, sluggish, confused and listless. A person might be holding their key yet still ask, "Where is the key?"

This stage is equivalent to the stage of the youth, when you are swayed by emotions, bewildered by them; when you begin to feel there is more to be known and you are somehow ignorant, it's a state beyond the fickleness of the child. A mind in *mudha* is still unprepared for spiritual training but is not as disturbed as in the *ksipta* state.

VIKSIPTA - Here the mind receives information but seems unable to process it. The mind oscillates in confusion, with an inner chatter like, "I want to do everything, but I can't do everything. Should I do this or that?" So you are preoccupied or infatuated. *Viksipta* is the state of someone possessed by an idea, by love, by ambition. No longer a confused youth, but a person with a clear aim, and an idea that possesses him or her.

It may be either the fixed idea of the madman, or the fixed idea that makes the hero or the saint, but in any case he is possessed by the idea. The quality of the idea and whether it is true or not is what makes the difference between the madman and the hero.

Either way, when you are under the spell of a fixed idea, when your mind is caught up on it, no reasoning can change it, for that change requires more openness in the mind and it is not available in this state.

Viksipta signifies a mind that is easily distracted, although when in this state you can achieve some degree of concentration of the mind but it gets distracted all too easily and too often. So this mind is mostly wandering, but steady on occasions, and that steadiness requires a lot of effort.

EKAGRA - In this state, the mind is relaxed but not sleepy, sharp but not stuck. You are ready to focus and pay attention, which is a prerequisite to meditation. A good yoga class can bring the mind into this state of relaxed attention.

At the previous state the idea possesses the person, but now the person possesses the idea, we are at that one-pointed state of the mind called *Ekagra* in Sanskrit.

A mature person, ready for the true life will be in *ekagra*. This state signifies the mind has achieved one-pointed concentration by virtue of prolonged and repeated practice. It is a peaceful, very pleasant state of mind. When you are at this stage you can concentrate easily and for extended periods of time. Here, concentration is not forced as in *viksipta* but comes effortlessly and naturally.

In the third stage, *viksipta*, where you are possessed by the idea, you are learning *Vivekah* or discrimination between the outer and the inner, the real and the unreal. When you have learned the lesson of *Vivekah*, advanced a stage forward, and in *ekagra* you choose one idea (in yoga this is the inner life), fix your mind on that idea, learn *Vairagya* or detachment/dispassion. Then you'll rise above the desire to possess objects of enjoyment, belonging either to this or any other world. Then you will advance towards the fifth stage.

NIRUDDHA – Mind Mastery

Here the mind is not distracted by random thoughts but is fully absorbed in the object of focus. This can
144

occur in meditation or when a person is fully engaged in something.

Niruddha means 'Master Mind'. It signifies a mind that is completely under control and functions without getting distracted or upset. It is really a state beyond the mind, a thoughtless state.

A person who has attained *niruddha* will almost spontaneously be able to enter into deep meditation. Niruddha is the result of tireless, competent spiritual practice and the fruit and culmination of spiritual training.

Examine your mind in order to recognise these stages in yourself. Can you choose your idea and cling to it of your own will, or do the ideas that the external world throws at you disturb you too much to remain focus on your own ideas and goals?

If you can choose your idea and stay with it, concentrating without being disturbed, then short is the step from that to complete control, which can inhibit all movements of the mind. When you reach that stage, and continue to practice, then it is only natural to pass into *samadhi* – total control of the mind.

When you understand how the different states of mind can be identified, and then derive from this the tools, techniques and practices needed to improve the current state, with the main goal being the ultimate state, then you have the key to coping with, benefiting from and growing because of change.

Understanding the different states of mind, developing *Shraddha*, *Vivekah* and *Vairagya* will ultimately make you more agile and accepting of inevitable change and will empower you and the business to inspire innovative performance.

System 7 – Tree of Wisdom™

The Tree of wisdom™ is derived from another system of yoga that comes directly from Patanjalis yoga sutras. The five *Kleshas*, which means impediments or hangups. The root is to be without knowledge, so we are ignorant *(Avidya)*, when we are ignorant we feel separate (Asmita), and when we feel separate we have a lot of judgements and likes *(Raga)* and dislikes *(Dvesha)*, because we are trying to join back in with the tribe or we want to become significant and outstanding to the point of acceptance. But our likes and dislikes drive us into fear *(Abhinivesha)*. We are frightened that we won't get any more of what we like. We are frightened that we will get more of what we don't like. This results in our feeling isolated and more separate, we collaborate less, we communicate less. Relationships may become unravelled; any innovation is lost, people won't move out of their box because they are as if frozen in fear.

Using The Tree of Wisdom™ to help understand what is at the root of the fear, and to realise that although it is also necessary to be an individual that does not negate you're still part of the whole, you do have your individual tasks and responsibilities to take care of.

How to find this clarity of perspective, this vision from a higher place is to go inside the mind and view objectively the different states of mind. The different states of mind identified in yoga are: the monkey mind. It just hops around, 'oh thought, oh another thought, oh bright shinny thing, oh where did I come from, I'll go back there', and it jumps around like a monkey in a cage, *Kshipta*, restless mind, and if the mind is not active, we end up with a *Mudha* mind. A listless mind is full of *tamas*, it's too heavy, it's got no life. The monkey mind has got too much *Rajas*. Then you get the distracted mind, *viksipta,* which is a bit of both.

If you start to understand what happens with these, you can gain some balance and become focused. When you can focus your mind, that's when you get your work done, and that's when you are able to generate great achievements, and are able to focus and concentrate, find solutions and get things done.

When you learn how to manage and focus your mind in such a way that you can do it at will, for as long as you need to, and it's absolutely under your control, you then have a controlled mind that goes where you want it to go.

Those are the different states of mind, and they are important because we want to help people to learn how to get to focused and then into control.

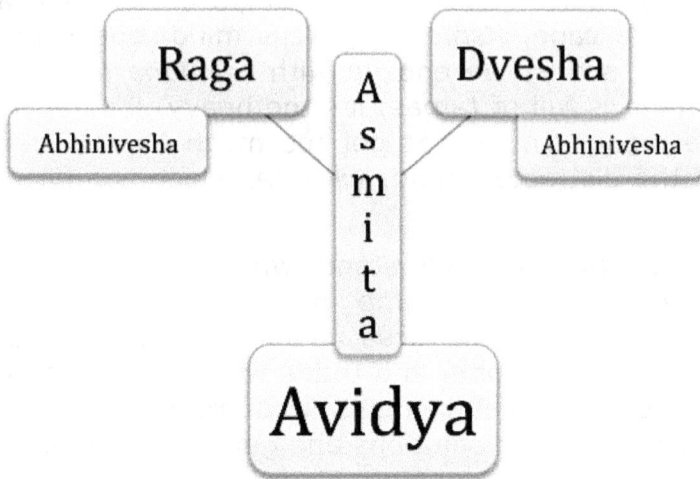

The Five Afflictions - *Kleshas*

1. Avidya – Ignorance, the root

2. Asmita – Ego, the trunk

3. Raga – Attachment, the branch

4. Dvesha – Repulsion, the branch

5. Abhinivesha – Fear, the fruit

The prime cause of the mental and emotional afflictions is spiritual ignorance, a lack of knowledge called *avidya*. Unfortunately this ignorance is primeval for so many. They have no idea of their authentic true self or their potential. They assume that their essence is mundane. It is by finding teachings that offer some truth that you can get some idea about this essential authentic self. You begin to recognise this ego, the misplaced self-identity *asmita* and how "it" causes so much pain, numerous afflictions - *dukham*.

If you attach your psychological energy to people and things in a harmful way there will be *dukham*. It is through the discipline of yoga that you develop the power to control the sense of identity, so that focuses only on higher realities and ultimately brings *Sukham*.

The tendency for emotional attachment *raga* is an impulse that is curbed after you have mastered *pratyahara* the fifth of the *astanga* eight limbs. It is a result of all of the previous practices and is a withdrawing of the senses or sensual energies from their external habitual focus. It conserves energy within the psyche which is then available and needed for meditation.

The opposite of *raga* compulsion is *dvesha* and is repulsion. It is impulsivity, these two *kleshas* are the result of our individual self interacting with the material world, our likes – *raga,* and our dislikes - *dvesha* and we can get so caught up in these and use them to define our identity, this feels hard wired at first and is hard to control. But through yoga you can find this control and gain an understanding, an awareness of how the strong focus on mundane existence, is due to an instinctive fear (ultimately of death) *abhinivesah* and this whole structure is removed by the realisation of the true self.

Practicing yogic techniques that encourage *pratyahara* means you find yourself in your subtle body, separated from the gross material one, gradually eroding the instinctive fear of death and any necessity to focus only on material existence, brining balance and light to your inner self.

System 8 – Supra Consciousness Access Channel™

The Eight Limbs of Yoga		
Astanga Yoga		
Sanskrit Word	**Translation**	**Description**
1 Yama	Universal morality and Restraints	Behaviour toward others (don'ts)
2. Niyama	Observances	Behaviour toward yourself (do's)
3. Asana	Posture	Position/disposition of the body, mind and feelings.
4. Pranayama	Breath Control	Movement of life force and emotions
5. Pratyahara	Introversion	Withdrawal of the senses, Looking within
6. Dharana	Concentration	Focus & concentration of energies
7 Dhyana	Meditation	Meditative state of stillness
8. Samadhi	Equilibrium	Unified state of mind, equanimity, ultimate freedom and endless joy

Things you do (spans rows 1–4)

Things that happen to you (spans rows 5–8)

Creating the mindset that's fit for the flexible business of the future. (And the body fit for a leotard!)

In this system of eight limbs, the different aspects are devised in a cohesive way, that when used together will achieve the desired objective. It can be considered a scientific method for Self-Realisation (Patanjali calls it *Samadhi*); each step leads to the next; acting as a preparation for the following step. If any of those steps is by-passed, it will adversely affect the whole process.

We compartmentalise or selves, our businesses, our problems, our lives, our behaviours, our beliefs. This is how we've been educated, to isolate an issue and attack it full on. Sadly this doesn't work, in any aspect of life this goes against our authentic higher nature, our true nature. We are an organism, and organisation of cells, so by compartmentalising we stop considering parts of the whole, those parts continue to exert their power through their inherent connections to the whole.

People often practice Yoga without attending to all of these eight steps, the method clearly defined by Patanjali - and they ultimately fail.

"When you see a good person, think of becoming like her/him. When you see someone not so good, reflect on your own weak points."

- Confucius

The goal of Yoga is Self-Realisation Samadhi. When you achieve it's heady heights, you shine out as the bright star that you truly are... To us beginners this goal may seem difficult to understand, but I'm sure you have witnessed being in the presence of (or seeing on the screen) a person who you admire, someone authentic, charismatic, compassionate, open hearted, open minded and knows themselves so well they are filled with self confidence, self esteem, self love – self realisation!

It is possible to have a very strong and healthy body, by continuously practicing *asanas* and *pranayamas*; but this strong and healthy state will not necessarily help promote a calm, strong and clear mind, it may look great in your leotard – if you have gone for that option! However, if you don't bring the mind under control, will you never be able to sustain the enjoyment of being so strong and healthy? Control of the mind is the first stop on route to Samadhi.

In the same way; sitting for hours in meditation, or going on long retreats and sitting for days in silence... and still you don't succeed reaching your goals. You see, if your moral, ethical and mental attitudes and behaviours have not been previously controlled by the first and preparatory steps of *Astanga*, steps known as Observances (*Yamas* and *Niyamas*) then the physical and breathing exercises will not build and sustain the required mindset.

Shri Yogendraji, one of my most honoured teachers, once compared the Eight Fold Path with the eight components of a chemical experiment. "You want to obtain a certain substance, and you have been provided a formula, wherein the eight elements must be put together. You must attend to the formula, for if

152

you fail in adding any of the ingredients, the whole experiment will be a failure."

Everything can be achieved in Yoga. Health, strength, flexibility, clarity, focus, concentration and even enlightenment. But only if this eight fold path is properly understood and attended to.

Authentic leadership is becoming more frequently recognised as a vital part of modern management science. Understanding how to use all of this great wisdom to benefit an organisation comes when we look at the link between leadership, authenticity and mindset. Authenticity has been explored throughout history, including Greek philosophers and the work of Shakespeare.

> *"To thy own self be true."*
>
> –Polonius, Hamlet (Shakespeare)

Authentic leaders display those higher human needs described by Maslow in chapter 6. They are self-aware, genuine and self-actualised individuals who are aware of their strengths, their limitations, and their emotions. They also show their real selves to their followers. They don't act one way in private and another in public; they don't hide their mistakes or weaknesses out of fear of looking weak. They also realise that being self-actualised is an endless journey, never complete.

Authentic leaders are mission driven and at the same time focused on results. They are able to put the mission and the goals of the organisation as a whole ahead of their own self-interest. They are doing job in pursuit of results, and not for their own power, money or ego.

They lead with their heart, not just their minds. They are not afraid to show their emotions, their vulnerability and to connect with their employees. This does not mean authentic leaders are "soft." In fact communicating in a direct manner is critical to successful outcomes, but it's done with empathy; directness without empathy is cruel.

They focus on the long-term value and are not blinkered or limited to short tem endeavours and beating quarterly estimates! Realising that to nurture individuals and to nurture a company requires hard work and patience, but the approach pays large dividends over time.

This desired mindset may require a total reconditioning of attitude and behaviour pattern towards life and that is what these eight steps do.

Yamas

Personal values and restraints. There are five steps here that guide you in modifying your behaviour so you reduce or remove dis-ease. These are the don'ts and refer to your behaviour towards others.

They include concepts that encourage honesty, integrity, humility and modesty.

Niyamas

Social morals and ethics. Once you understand what values, morals and ethics drive and motivate you, and you study and regulate yourself and your behaviours.

These are the do's and refer to how you behave towards yourself.

Supporting the development of the ability to judge ethical dilemmas and other issues from multiple perspectives. Foster self-awareness, discipline and capacity to regulate things like internal self-talk. Brining greater levels of self-clarity so you are more aware of you core beliefs and possess greater courage to act in accordance with your deeply held values.

I am continuously surprised by how many leaders attempt to act at being something they are not and be one way at work, while their "true" personality emerges outside of work.

You may have heard that "Leadership is acting." But is this absolutely true? I have witnessed and been surprised by leaders who seem shocked or confused when their employees don't trust them, don't like them, and can't wait to work elsewhere.

"If you and I are having a single thought of violence or hatred against anyone in the world at this moment, we are contributing to the wounding of the world."

Deepak Chopra

Asana

This is the part of yoga that most people think of as all of yoga – the physical exercises, stretches and postures.

Asana actually means, 'How do you feel sitting inside yourself? Are you feeling comfortable, do you feel like you are in a comfort zone inside yourself, even when your body is out of its comfort zone? Can you feel comfortable in your body standing on your head? Can you feel comfortable in your body with your legs tied in knots! Because if you can, it means you can then begin to cope with more and more difficult situations.

Pranayama

With that, we then move into breath. The breath is the bridge between the body and the mind. Now you've got your morals and your ethics aligned and you are happy with them, you are able to sit happily in your comfortable body.

If you can manage the breath, keep it rhythmic and controlled, then you will automatically be able to keep the mind calm and focused and controlled. So the breath is the bridge to the mind.

We teach you how to focus on the breath because you can't think and focus on the breath at the same time. It's impossible to think and feel at the same time, so by focusing on the breath, you learn how to stop your thoughts. This takes you to the final four stages, the internal steps.

Pratyahara

The first internal stage is withdrawing the senses inside, you stop noticing anything external and the senses then don't need any of your energy. This happens to you when you become proficient at pranayama and concentrating on the breath.

Dharana

The second internal stage then happens while continuing to concentrate on the breath, the mind just has to stop and go quiet, the breath (or the single object chosen as the focus) is the only focus of the mind, this is the same as the state called ekagra, one-pointed.

Dhyana

The third internal stage is realising the mind has gone quiet and allowing it to stay there so now the mind is as if looking into itself.

Samadhi

The final stage is realising there is an observer and the universal consciousness is behind all this and that's what you are: an observer. From here this is really seeing the bigger picture, like God's eye view!

You are universal consciousness. You are a little reflection of the universal consciousness and that's called *Samadhi*. That observer, that witness, is the goal of the eight limbs of yoga.

> "We are not a drop in the ocean;
> we are the ocean in a drop."
>
> -Rumi

When you are in the position of being the witness, you feel totally balanced and harmonious in any situation. This is where the hatha yoga can be understood because polarities, hot and cold, good and bad, black and white, dark and light – all the polarities stop interfering with you, how you feel and how you behave. You are centred and grounded in consciousness. It is here that tantra and hatha yoga all come together. Tantrically, you want to stay centred and grounded. Whether you are happy or sad, you are centred and grounded. Beyond happiness is this bliss. *Ananda* is bliss. In this the supreme mind-state, you have mastered the skill of accessing supra consciousness.

Evolve

Evolution comes out of expansion, so to expand your people, their capabilities, their authenticity, their abilities and their resilience. To allow and facilitate the expansion of the leadership through innovation, creativity, into ingenious - will expand your company into flourishing sustainable profitability.

Resulting in energised, empowered, and evolved processes, people, leaders and the whole organisation.

System 9 – Perception Expansion Program ™

This program begins by looking into the mind at the ways that it perceives, because the way you perceive affects everything about who you are. If you expand your perception, you naturally expand your being. Through your perception, you observe and identify things. You perceive things and sometimes you get it right, other times you perceive things wrongly.

If you open up your understanding, identifying that there are five levels at which perception work, you can at the same time expand the mind by understanding what's inside each one. Then in turn you can begin to witness and become an objective observer of your own perception and no longer a victim of it.

As you grow there is constantly learning and your limitations will change. Every time you peel a layer off, it's like a snakeskin and you are a little bit more expanded. From there you can go through and look for the next layer of limitations.

Of all the countless thoughts, impressions and perceptions that come into the mind, they all fall into one or more of these five categories. In other words, while there are many individual thoughts, there only five types of thoughts to consider. This can help in seeing the underlying simplicity of the process of Yoga, not getting lost in the apparent complexity.

Patanjali calls these *vrittis,* whirlwinds or mental objects, and here are the five he states:

1. *pramana* = real or valid cognition, right knowledge, valid proof, seeing clearly

2. *viparyayah* = unreal cognition, indiscrimination, perverse cognition, wrong knowledge, misconception, incorrect knowing, not seeing clearly

3. *vikalpah* = imagination, verbal misconception or delusion, fantasy, hallucination

4. *nidra* = deep sleep

5. *smritayah* = memory, remembering

Witnessing the five kinds of thoughts and learning to observe the thinking process, you can discriminate *(viveka)* between these five types *vrittis,* you start to gain a mastery over them, and their ability to control your actions, speech, and thoughts.

As mastery comes closer you gradually find a detached *(Vairagya) state* of witnessing, where you can observe the entire flow of mind, while remaining peacefully undisturbed, unaffected, and uninvolved. Meditation can systematically deepen.

Without that mastery, you remain a victim of your own unconscious mental process, losing free choice in external life as well as the ability to experience deep meditation.

Pramana is the one to cultivate, and is the one we focus on in the Productive Perception Processor™. *Pramana*, or correct knowledge is the process of continually seeing more and more clearly, it brings progress on the path of meditation. This process of seeing clearly, of seeing things as they are, is one of the ways of describing the inner journey, eventually revealing that absolute, unchanging authentic and True Self.

Pramana
right
knowledge

Smritayah
memory

Viparyaya
wrong
knowledge

Pancha
Vrittis

Nidra
sleep

Vikalpa
imagination

System 10 – Supra Conscious Success system ™

This system enables true mastery, and that could be personal mastery of your own business, leadership mastery of the business you work in, or company business mastery for planning, performance and profit.

All levels of being including; physical, mental, psychosomatic, sensory, intellectual, emotional or spiritual are categorised into *bhavas*. *Bhava* means attitude. There are Eight in total, four positive and four negative. The positive ones are *dharma* (self direction), *jnana* (knowledge that wholesome, fulfilling & calming), *vairagya* (creating larger understanding and healthy objective distance to encourage letting go) and *aishwariya* (self-reliance, will power). The four negative ones are *adharma* (lack of self direction), *ajnana* (lack of wisdom), *raga* (attachment) and *unaishwariya* (lack of will power).

What is your attitude toward what you do?

If you continuously feel disharmonious especially about actions you do perform then how can you bring balance back into your life?

Life is to celebrate and be celebrated

The first one is *Dharma*; knowing what you need to do now in this present moment, doing your duty.

The second is *Jnana*, which is knowledge. You must learn something in order to do what it is you have to do right now, so you learn how to do it.

The third is *Vairagya* – You're doing and you can drop the knowledge, because you've learnt it. You don't need to think about it anymore. Take riding a bike for instance. With *Dharma*, you want to ride a bike. *Jnana*, learn to ride a bike. *Vairagya*, is like doing tricks. You don't even know how you are doing it anymore because you have forgotten what you learnt. You have let it go and the performance is happening.

Then there is *Aishwariya*, the feeling of self-esteem, fulfilment, self-confidence, magnificence, appreciation – of all of the things that come when you do bicycle tricks and you win first prize.

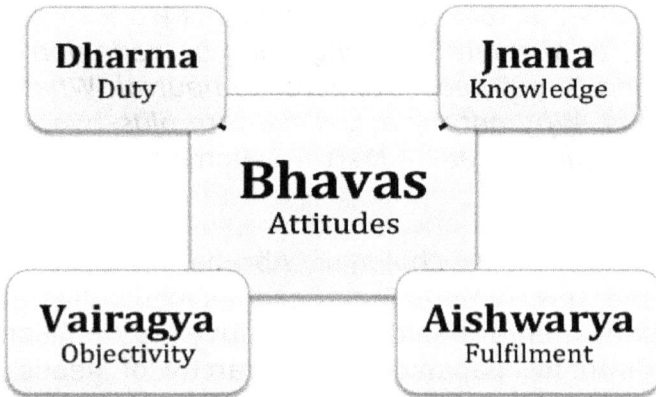

Dharma Duty	**Jnana** Knowledge
Bhavas Attitudes	
Vairagya Objectivity	**Aishwarya** Fulfilment

That is the PRIME Profit Paradigm™

To build a good business, You must know what you ought to do. You learn how to do it. You practice doing it and do it until you can detach from the results as well as the learning – which is where many yoga practices and exercises take you - into *Vairagya*. From here comes this feeling of *Aishwariya*. You will have this feeling of wow, we've grown, we're making profits, not even the sky is the limit!

Chapter 6

The Transformation

The Psychology of Human Behaviour, Motivation and Needs.

I believe psychology has done very well in working out how to understand and treat disease. But I think that is literally half-baked. If all you do is work to fix problems, to alleviate suffering, then by definition you are working to get people to zero, to neutral. What I'm saying is, Why not try to get them to plus-two, or plus-three? – Martin Seligman.

Another American Psychologist, Abraham Maslow, was one of the few famous American psychologists who wrote about mental health in a positive way – "Mental strength". In his paper titled "Hierarchy of needs", a theory on human motivation, he offers a model that helps to explain how human motivation and human needs are organised and inter-related. He stated: "What is necessary to change a person is to change his awareness of himself."

Maslow's Hierarchy of Needs

Maslow says every human has a hierarchy of needs. For the top need he uses the term "Self Actualised", which correlates closely to the Yogic term "Self Realisation".

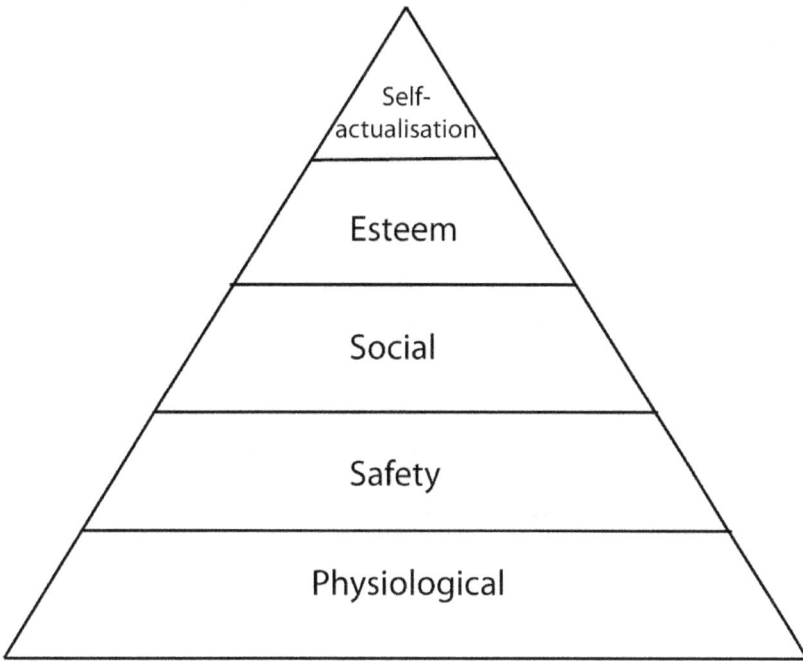

A triangle diagram divided into five horizontal levels, from top to bottom: Self-actualisation, Esteem, Social, Safety, Physiological.

Maslow's masterpiece "A hierarchy of human needs" is based on two groupings:

> A) Deficiency needs, and

> B) Growth needs.

A) Within the deficiency needs 1-4, each lower need must be met before moving to the next higher level. The first four levels are:

> 1. Physiological

> 2. Safety/security

> 3. Connection

4. Esteem

B) According to Maslow, an individual is ready to attend to the growth needs if and only if the deficiency needs are met. His initial concept included only one growth need:

    5. Self-actualisation: (personal growth and fulfilment)

Maslow says that people who are self-actualised have the following characteristics: problem-focused; appreciation of life; concerned with personal growth; able to have peak experiences.

After his initial papers on this subject, Maslow later split the growth need of self-actualisation, specifically identifying two of the first growth needs as part of the more general level of self-actualisation, and one beyond the general level that focused on growth beyond that oriented towards self. They are:

- Cognitive: knowledge, understanding, and exploration;

- Aesthetic: symmetry, order, and beauty;

- Self-actualisation: to find self-fulfilment and realise your potential; and

- Self-transcendence: to connect to something beyond the ego or to help others find self-fulfilment and realise their potential.

Maslow's Hierarchy of Human Needs

1. Physiological need – the most basic of our human needs: food, water, warmth, shelter, sleep etc. Maslow argued that unless physiological needs are satisfied to some degree, no other motivating factor can actually work.

2. Safety or security need – the need to be free of physical danger and emotional harm, so here you can consider the fear of losing a job, property, food or shelter. It relates to security, protection and stability in the events of everyday life.

3. Social Need – the needs for love, affection, connection and social acceptance. We are social beings and as such will always try to satisfy our needs for acceptance and friendship.

4. Esteem – once your social needs are satisfied you look for esteem (reputation and significance). This need produces a sense of satisfaction from power, prestige, status and self-confidence. It includes both internal esteem factors like self-respect, autonomy and achievements, and external esteem factors such as recognition, approval and attention as well as a personal sense of competence.

5. Self-actualisation – the drive to reach your maximum potential or peak performance. It includes growth and self-fulfilment by achieving and fulfilling your potential to accomplish something.

Tony Robbins' Six Human Needs Psychology

Tony Robbins, an inspirational and motivation speaker and success coach, has been ranked among the "Top

50 Business Intellectuals in the World" by Accenture's Institute for Strategic Change, and was ranked by Harvard Business School to be among the "Top 200 Business Gurus".

Amongst Robbins' pearls of wisdom is this:
"Most people have no idea of the giant
capacity we can immediately command when
we focus all of our resources on mastering a
single area of our lives".

This model identifies six human needs and, as with Maslow's model, is based on the premise that human motivation can be explained by means of these universal human needs:

1. Certainty (safety/security) – everybody wants stability when it comes to their basic necessities of food, shelter and other physical material resources. In addition, everyone needs a basic sense of security about family, finances, work and relationships.

2. Uncertainty/Variety (physiological) – if life was only full of certainty we would get bored and more importantly we wouldn't evolve or grow. We all have a need to change our state, to exercise the body and emotions. Therefore, we seek variety through a number of means: a change of scene, physical activity or stimuli, mood swings, entertainment, food. Too much brings fear, especially when relating to the previous need, but too little brings boredom and stagnation.

3. Significance (esteem) – everybody needs to feel special and important in some way. Seeking

significance by getting recognition from others or from ourselves, maybe by becoming a high achiever. If we feel insignificant, we may make ourselves feel significant by getting angry or by putting others down, so we feel like we are better than them. We may also meet this need paradoxically, by having others recognise the significance of our insignificance. Another popular vehicle is acting/dressing in an eccentric way. Many people take pride in being different and unique for that's what fulfils their need for significance. But if we strive for too much significance and uniqueness, we end up totally different than everyone else, which violates the next need.

4. Connection/Love (social) – Humans need to feel connected with someone or something: a person, an ideal, a value, a habit, a sense of identity. Connection may take the form of love or merely of intense engagement – for instance, it's possible to feel connected by engaging in an aggressive interaction. The core of all human connections are based on similarities or sameness with one another, so beware of being too busy striving for significance, as we won't feel connected, we'll feel alone and disjointed from people. But by being too connected we may lose our own identity and violate our need for significance.

5. Growth (self-actualisation) – everything in the universe is either growing or dying, there is no third alternative. We will not be spiritually satisfied unless our capacities are expanding. Many people's goal is to reach a certain financial target, or style of life, but when they get there, they become stagnant. While others might envy what these people have or

achieve, they themselves are unhappy because they aren't growing anymore. We all need something to strive for, something that'll challenge us to grow and take our lives to the next level.

6. Contribution (self-actualisation) – just as we can't survive without others contributing in some way to our welfare (no baby grew up on its own), we can't be spiritually fulfilled unless we are contributing to others as well. Aside from ourselves, we all desire to make a difference and contribute to the greater good. In essence everything must serve a purpose in the big ecosystem. So we as human beings all have a deep desire to contribute outside of ourselves.

Even though all of us have the same basic human needs, the order of importance varies. For some, security might be essential, while for others it's variety or significance.

As with Maslow's model, the first four are primary biological drives that must be met in some form. Robbins makes it clear that these basic personal needs can be met either through positive or negative behaviour. The human nervous system will interpret both as a way of meeting those needs.

To make progress, we must find positive ways of meeting personal needs and by moving beyond the first four, which are the needs of the personality, to the last two needs, growth and contribution, which are a source of spiritual satisfaction.

Human Needs Viewed With Pancha Kosha

The *pancha koshas* can be compared to and understood by relating them to the five human needs of Maslow's model.

To gain a deeper understanding of human suffering we must understand Self and non-Self.

Human existence is depicted and understood in terms of a multi-layered organisation. In the *pancha kosha* model, the idea of Self is of a conscious being and not of a reactive organism.

It is our identification with the mind-body complex, the reactive organism, that prevents us from realising our true nature, a conscious being that is represented by our soul (*Atman*). Once we develop an understanding of the five *koshas*, we slowly peel off these layers and this brings us closer to our true identity.

The concept of the *pancha kosha* provides a useful framework for understanding the mind-body complex in an experiential way. *Pancha* means "five" and *kosha* means "body" or "sheath". A human being is seen as being composed of five overlapping *koshas*.

The concept of inner awareness really is at the foundation of yoga teachings. Usually you only become aware of what is going on inside of you when life and your experiences give rise to feelings of pain or pleasure.

Yoga enables development of a heightened and refined sensitivity to your inner world of sensations and a capacity for focused attention. When you have developed these skills you can bring a wide range of inner activities into your field of awareness. Only through this awareness can you begin to regulate, balance and harmonise yourself from the inside out.

Pancha Kosha

1. Annamayakosha; Physiological - food and nourishment
2. Pranamayakosha; Safety or Security – breath and energy
3. ManoMayaKosha; Social – sensations and emotions
4. Vijnanamayakosha; Esteem – ego and intellect
5. Anandamayakosha; Self actualisation – Self or atma

As a human being, the most primordial and basic need is to keep the body going, to nourish and fuel it with food. The food body *annamayakosha* primarily needs food and water for survival.

Annamayakosha (physical body)

This is the field of the ordinary, everyday consciousness. Your awareness is focused on sensations that result from the contact of your physical body with the outside world. There are two parts to this:

(a) Sense organs and sensory receptors of the body, extero-receptors

(b) Perception of yourself as person in the form of the physical body.

Normally, over-activity at this level tends to drown out other forms of sensation happening 'from the inside', what your potential, your limitations and your true nature are.

Pranamayakosha (energy body)

In yoga, you slowly develop the capacity to disengage from the overwhelming sensations coming from the extero-receptors, and pay attention to the subtle internal sensations coming from the entero-receptors. This is the field of the *pranamayakosha*, which provides a link between the body (*annamayakosha*) and the mind (*manomayakosha*).

Through this process of disengaging, you become aware that identifying the Self as just the body is not only partial but frequently leads to a distortion of your self image. The true nature of the Self is quite different from the image perceived in this ordinary way. We are not only what we see in the mirror.

The practices of *asana* and *pranayama* help you to develop internal awareness of sensations that arise from within the body:

• enteroceptive – sensing mechanical or chemical stimulation

• proprioceptive – sensing where the different body parts are in space

• kinesthetic – sensing body position, temperature, weight and movement

• visceroceptive - senses associated with changes in viscera (organs)

The main function of *Pranamayakosha* is to support and energise the subtle body. *Prana* can be translated as the energy, and is often understood as breath, although *prana* more correctly means subtle bio-energy and the breath is just the gross movement of air in and out of the body. There is a direct relationship between the way the body energy

173

behaves or is modified when the breath is modified, *pranayama*. *Prana* travels through *nadis* (channels), which are conduits for the energy to move to all parts of the body and to different organs to keep the body functioning. We can understand *prana* as the electricity needed to run the material body. The *pranamayakosha* can be looked upon as being responsible for all the physiological functions in the body: breathing, blood circulation, digestion, heartbeat, all hormonal functions and the transmission of neural electrical impulses that allow communication between the brain and the cells of the body.

Manomayakosha (lower mind, emotional body)

This is the field of consciousness that interprets sensory input (both internal and external) and carries out many of our normal mental functions e.g. control of movements, instinctual responses, simple forms of rational thinking and ordinary emotions. Many of the activities from this level are relatively blind and automatic, leading to many of life's problems.

Manomayakosha is the level where we make sense of and try to understand what happens to us – what we perceive through the senses. We develop an emotive ability of determining and fulfilling all of our basic drives and desires. This includes love, compassion and understanding the other, the need for company, companionship and connection.

Manomaya means "made up of", which is mind. So it's all the thinking, cognising, feeling and willing. Using the information provided by the five sensory organs, we interpret whether what we perceive is good or bad, our likes and dislikes. This is the part of the mind that tends to be full of its own importance.

174

Likes and dislikes create our desires, so this *kosha* is much more powerful than the preceding two and it governs them. It is, in turn, governed by the next two *koshas*, hence it is central to human existence, and is why we use the word 'man' (from *manas*) to represent human.

Many therapeutic modalities and treatments work at this level. Aromatherapy, music and colour therapy, placebo and even homeopathic medicines in the higher potencies influence this *Kosha*.

Pranamayakosha, described above, is directly influenced by our mind. When we are agitated, stressed or angry our breathing is fast, shallow and irregular. When we are calm and peaceful, our breathing is also calm and regular.

Manomayakosha is responsible for our cognitive abilities, communicating with the intellect and directing our actions, thoughts and emotions. Memories are also a part of the mind.

Every thought has a great inherent power; it affects our physiology, moods, physical body, reactions, responses, work efficiency, relationships and even wisdom.

The modern day epidemic of stress and being as it were stuck in fight or flight is a problem at the level of mind, because always being stressed out causes a build up of strong negative emotion that is never released or vented.

Patanjali, in his yoga sutras, defines yoga as the ability to control the fluctuations or movements in the mind, and that only through controlling the mind can we experience our true inner peace and joy. He also tells us that the main techniques needed to attaining this peaceful and joyful state are steps five, six and seven of the eight-step Astanga. They are *pratyahara* (sense withdrawal), *dharana* (concentration) and *dhyana* (meditation). Patanjali states that regular, uninterrupted practice of meditation, done with a sense of total devotion, will bring about a total transformation in your personality and provide lasting peace and freedom from stress.

Vijnanamayakosha (higher mind, intellectual body)

This is the level of higher intellect, the more refined or higher emotions and intuition.

Awareness at this level extends beyond that of ordinary self-consciousness and leads us to act for the greater good, not self-centred but from a higher or a universal sense of interconnectedness.

Emotions at this level are qualitatively different from those of the manomayakosha. For instance, love is expansive, unconditional and without motive or concern for yourself. As a result your thoughts and actions are qualitatively different.

This is the body of the intellect (*buddhi*), intuitive knowledge and wisdom. It gives us the discriminative capability that helps us distinguish the difference between a) basic likes and dislikes, and b) fundamental good and evil or right and wrong.

The intellect can be looked upon as having two components; one that is controlled by our ego and driven by our past memories and impressions/habits (*samskaras*), and the other that is controlled by our pure intuition. The ego-driven intellect can lead to actions that result in pain and suffering while actions

176

driven by pure intuition will give us satisfaction and happiness.

Buddhi is a product of universal knowledge (*Mahat*). It contains all the necessary ingredients needed to reach self-actualisation. In its perfected form it is said to quicken learning and evolution that leads to you reaching your optimum potential. Patanjali states that the practice of yoga – defined as control and management of the *Buddhi* – brings both self-actualisation and self-realisation.

Using a concept known as the four *Bhavas* (latent states of the subconscious) to guide us in our own education and personal development, we can ensure that as individuals we not only grow to reach our own fullest potential but also contribute to the furthering of the community's progress.

Vijnanamayakosha is where the integrating and refining processes of yoga take place. Through re-collection and meditation a sharp discriminative faculty is developed, leading to awareness of processes of the higher and lower mind, in the *manomayakosha* and in the *vijnanamayakosha* itself. This, combined with the enhanced awareness of the processes in the *pranamaya* and *manomaya koshas*, enables us to intelligently correct our own self-image, our behaviours and our attitudes and the integrating and refining of the whole person.

Without these integrating and refining processes defined in yoga, the Ego, this sense of I as a separate entity, can become dominant and yoga attributes this to the cause of much if not all of our suffering. In all the previous levels or bodies, we are unaware of our so-called Ego. It is only through the functioning of this body, *vijnanamayakosha*, that we are able to learn about the individual self, the Ego.

Through the practice of meditation our mind becomes purified, the intellect can then begin to depend more and more on the pure intuitive wisdom rather than be influenced by the Ego.

Anandamayakosha (universal consciousness, bliss body)

At this level all life is one and there are no separate entities. Also known as the "abode of universal bliss", it is the source of enlightenment.

The Sanskrit word *ananda* means "bliss" or "pure joy". When we transcend the other four layers described above, we can begin to experience a sense of pure joy that does not need any sensory input or any of the past experiences or impressions. It is of the present moment only, purely in the now.

Facilitated by practicing the *astanga*, the eight steps prescribed by Patanjali, energy flows from here to the *vijnanamayakosha* and brings wisdom, energy and a sense of purpose in life; this can then energise the lower levels. An inner transformation occurs that corrects the self-image, promotes general health and well-being, and develops the confidence and capacity for coping with stress.

Anandamayakosha is the "Sheath of Bliss" or the bliss body, and this is what can be related to "Self-actualisation" as stated by Maslow.

This is the most natural state of the human or the soul. There are no more needs to be fulfilled, no memories or impressions of the past and no dreams or projections of the future. We are said to have reached the absolute of who we are, a part of and connected to the ultimate reality.

The *Pancha Koshas* are the invisible or metaphorical bodies or layers that cover the individual soul or *Atman*. When different needs are met and satisfied, the *Atman* can discard the appropriate layers one by one and finally in *vijnanamayakosha* when the Ego is dropped the *Atman*, the Self, is complete.

This layer is the closest to our true Self, which is ever pure and ever unchanging. You can experience this bliss as a result of *samadhi*, the last of the eight limbs of Patanjali's yoga philosophy. You can only experience *Samadhi* through diligent, continuous and uninterrupted practice of the other seven limbs on a regular basis.

Chapter 7

The Practice

How the Science of Yogic Breathing Brings Brilliance

Here we put your brain under the microscope and discover just how to get blood out of a stone!

From the *Pancha Kosha* model of the five yogic bodies, there is information that helps us to understand how the *pranamayakosha* (energy body) is the bridge from the physical body to the subtle workings of the mind.

This bridge can be understood in scientific terms through our neurophysiology – our brain function.

The techniques that are used to balance and support this bridge are yogic breathing techniques, called *Pranayama*, chanting (which is simply breath and sound) and meditation.

There is so much clinical research being undertaken in this area and the advanced technologies available today have helped to develop many tools and modalities that make it easier to see more clearly just what is happening in the brain. Functional MRI (magnetic resonance imaging) is the best current modality for studying the brain behaviour directly during *Pranayama*, chanting and meditation practice.

The fact that the ancient yogis were able to identify functions and workings of, and relate how the brain and the mind operate, are astounding. They had access to this knowledge through direct experience, through their own experience over five thousand years ago. Without access to any of the advanced technologies we have today, simply through their constant and diligent practice, and the resulting repeated experiences they were able to develop clear systematic models, effective techniques and in-depth teachings to help us to manage our neurophysiology, enabling us to manage our emotional state as well as our physical and mental performance.

The source of our brilliance

it's no mystery!

In 2007 a Spanish golfer called Sergio Garcia played in the British Open. He played brilliantly throughout, holding the lead after each one of the first three rounds and carrying a three-shot lead over the rest of the field into the start of the fourth day. This final round began well and he had extended the lead to four shots when the problems began; his performance plummeted and he ended up in a play-off for the game, which he eventually lost.

Then in the 2008 PGA championship, there was a similar performance, with Sergio playing brilliantly until the final nine holes brought him another defeat. On that final day, his shot count for the final nine holes went up by ten on the previous day's count for the same nine holes. He was playing exactly the same holes but overnight he had somehow lost his ability to perform in the same brilliant way as he had on the previous day.

What was it that caused this dramatic change in his performance?

Why did he have this complete loss of form?

With all of the advances in neurobiology, we now know why this happens, why Sergio Garcia made exactly the same mistakes, and why he did not learn how to overcome this apparent loss of brilliance despite all the training and coaching he underwent.

Understanding this from a neuro-scientific perspective will reveal to us the secrets of how your system, your neurophysiology, works. Knowing this allows you take control, even when you are challenged and have stepped beyond your comfort zone, it is still vital that you remain passionate and competent so you can achieve your full potential.

We are all after the same goal: to improve. To improve our performance or our results in some way. It doesn't actually matter what kind of results we are talking about. This book is focusing on business performance and results, but the information I'm about to reveal to you can be applied equally from public speaking to sporting results, from academic performance to relationship performance and sexual performance.

To change results you have to focus on behaviour. You have to do things differently in order to get a different result.

In business most performance appraisals focus on what you've been doing and puts it into two categories:

1. Things that you've done really well

2. Things that are you not so good at (the polite way of putting it!)

The conclusion is obvious, you must do more of number 1 and less (or none) of number 2.

Sometimes this method works and you get a different result by shifting your focus. But more often it doesn't make much difference, or it only makes a difference for a short while and eventually things go back to normal. Or things go well only when the boss stands over that employee cracking the whip, making sure they do 1 and not 2.

Appraisals are necessary, but they are also insufficient. Even when people know what to do, sometimes they just don't do it.

If you really want to change performance permanently, to be driven and motivated, then it is not enough just to focus on the surface behaviours, we must delve deeper into the internal environment, to the roots of the behaviour to get to grips with what's on the inside of individuals and understand more about *why* people do what they do.

How you think determines what you do, and finding out what people think means asking questions; it can't be done by just observing their behaviour. You need to get to the finer details of what they think to achieve a change in the results that is likely to last.

This is just the next step, it's still not enough. There is something even more fundamental driving how people think: how they feel.

Thinking affects feeling and feeling affects thinking, going back and forth in a loop. The dominant factor is feeling. There is a huge body of neuro-scientific evidence that explains the reasons for this, but for now let's just say that if you want to change what people do, to change their behaviour, you've got to change their thinking and to change their thinking you actually have to change how they feel.

Feelings have much more impact on us than any advice or support we are given. So if you feel anxious before an exam, a meeting or an interview, then it's no good me saying to you, "Don't worry." You've probably experienced that that doesn't work! If you feel anxious you feel anxious and no amount of "don't worry" will help you – in fact it can even make you worse!

The crucial point here is change how you feel – but for a permanent sustainable change in behaviour that is still not enough! There is something even more fundamental driving how you feel: your raw emotion. So you've got to change the emotion in order to change feeling – then the thinking, then the behaviour.

Many of you reading this will now have the same question in your mind: "Isn't feeling the same as an emotion?" No, it's not.

Feelings and emotions are not the same thing. Frequently when we are asked how we feel, we respond by saying how we are thinking. This is often because we simply don't understand the question but also a cultural norm too; we are not taught about feeling so we may find it difficult to notice feelings and put them into words.

If you want to change the result by changing the behaviour there are multiple levels, and at the level of emotions it's still not enough. We need to go down even deeper to the more fundamental level of our human system – to the physiology.

Improved Performance Route

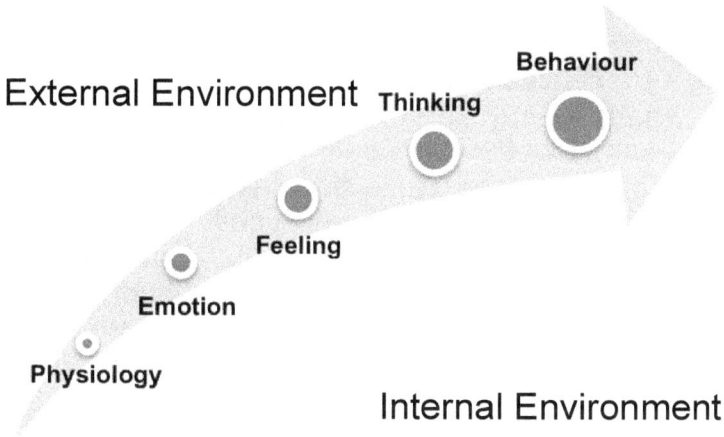

The reason for the variance in Sergio Garcia's performance is that there are multiple levels that he did not have control over, as is shown in the diagram above. He was just concentrating on his technical putting performance or the way he drives the ball, which is just his behaviour. He hadn't got to grips with any of the other levels. Even if he'd been telling himself, "I'm a good golfer, I'm a great golfer, I'm the best," rehearsing this mentally and so influencing his thinking, it would still not be deep enough. There are still three more levels that he hadn't got to grips with.

For consistent, sustainable, brilliant performance, you have got to learn how to control every level, and only then can you achieve optimal performance.

Working from the bottom to the top of the model, starting with physiology, what is that? It is simply streams of information, or data, travelling along nerve channels going to your brain and telling it what is going on in your body.

As you're reading this right now most of you are getting other streams of data coming into your brain about what's going on in your body. If you've just eaten you'll be getting a signal from your gut saying, "Mmm, we've got food"; this signal is telling your brain what's going on in your gut, and you'll have muscular contractions around the food, so you'll have pressure waves created telling the brain more about what's going on in your gut – this is physiology. When you consider all of the different functions that go on simultaneously in your body at any one time, it's a lot of data.

What's an emotion? If you take all the streams of data from your gut, your joints, your heart, your lungs etc, the data from all the streams from all the bodily systems as they enter your brain, there are electrical signals (nerve impulses), electromagnetic signals (energetic field interactions), chemical signals (hormones and neurotransmitters) and pressure waves (pressure). Take all of those signals from all of the body's systems and that is what an emotion is. It's simply energy, "e", in motion.

That's all an emotion is, a compound or combination of waves and signals. We all have emotions, every second of every day; there is an energetic state going through us, because we are constantly digesting, constantly breathing in and out, our hearts constantly beating, it's happening all the time.

Now even though we have energy in motion every single second of every single day, we may not all have feelings... the difference between emotions and feelings is awareness.

It All Starts With Awareness

Feelings are the awareness in our mind of that energy – and this can be a problem for some; the energy may be there but we are not aware of it, we don't feel it. If you look at a common experience for most people, at what is called an energetic signature of something like anxiety, showing what goes on physiologically when we're in a state of anxiety. Your heart rate is fast, your mouth is dry, it can be difficult to get your words out, the palms of the hands are sweaty and the gut is churning. These are the specific physiological constituents of that thing that you would know as "anxiety".

If I ask you how do you feel, and you say "Um, alright...", all that data is often there, the emotion is there, you're just not feeling it, not aware of it. However, even though you're not feeling it, it is still altering what you're thinking and how well you're thinking it, which is in turn changing what you're doing – but you don't realise this because you feel "alright". You're not noticing any of that, you're just thinking what you're thinking and doing what you're doing.

Consistent peak performance requires firstly awareness of what's happening internally, at the physiological and emotional levels, and secondly gaining control over it. If you are not aware of it you simply can't get control, so awareness is the first step. Many of the practices in yoga increase your awareness of your body and its feelings. When an *asana* is done properly it is done with complete awareness – where are your hands, shoulders, hips and feet? How are

187

they placed? What is happening to your breath? Can you keep your spine activated from top to bottom? There are many such instructions that you must follow in order to master the practice of *asana* and to do so you must develop awareness of your body.

Because most of us don't have the control at the physiological and emotional level it is impossible to maintain peak performance. In fact very few people do have control of any of this stuff on the internal environment. Even when people have been highly trained in regulating their behaviour, they still don't have much control of the inner levels.

This control is the source of your brilliance – if you can get control you can crank out your A game every single day.

What is it We Need to Control?

How do we decide which bit of the physiology to begin with? Given that there are so many different signals going to the brain, which one do we choose?

Neuroscientists have discovered that the heart directs many systems in the body and has its own independent nervous system, known as "the brain in the heart". The heart is in constant communication with the brain, scientists are discovering that our hearts may actually be the "intelligent force" behind the intuitive thoughts and feelings we all experience. So if we can create more balanced and coherent signals from the heart we will have a more positive influence over the brain.

Let's consider one specific signal: the electrical signal of the heart. Your heart beats, and makes its lovely beating sound. As the heart contracts it causes a spike of electricity that is received, as a signal, by the brain.

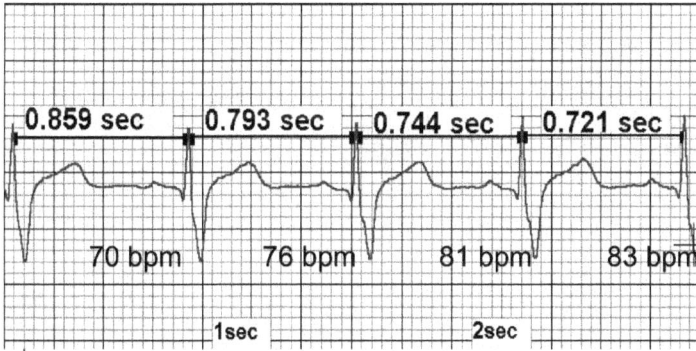

0.859 sec   0.793 sec   0.744 sec   0.721 sec

70 bpm   76 bpm   81 bpm   83 bpm

1sec   2sec

3.0 seconds of heart beat data

You can measure the time interval between each heartbeat, and this interval varies from beat to beat, which means the time between the electrical spikes produced by the contractions are different. But when a doctor takes your pulse he tells you the average is seventy, but in taking the average he's ignoring all the variance, and for the brain, it's the variance that really matters. Taking the average you lose all the critical data – it's like listening to Mozart and saying the average is

C# daaaaaaaaaaaaaaaaaaaaaaaaaaaaaaaa!

From the previous graph we can see that the average rate is 77.5, and if you look carefully you'll also see that each beat has its own individual signature.

This variance is called the heart rate variability (HRV) and is critical data for three reasons:

1. HRV accurately predicts your death (if we measure the HRV for twenty-four hours we can tell you when you're going to die).
2. HRV predicts how much energy you've got.
3. HRV alters brain function – this is the key to performance.

When we are happily getting on with life the HRV is quietly chaotic, as each and every beat is different, but not too different. But if we are put under pressure, our HRV becomes super chaotic.

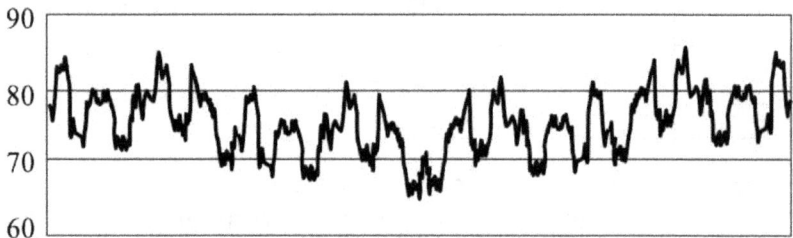

Chaotic HRV caused by anxiety

Your brain receives a signal that travels up the vagus nerve channel from the heart. In yogic terms the signal is the *prana* and the vagus nerve is the *nadi*. When you are under pressure this signal becomes chaotic, and the more pressure you are under the more chaotic it becomes.

The consequence of this chaotic signal is a shut down of the frontal lobes of the brain. The frontal lobes are responsible for decision-making, problem solving, judgements, planning, working memory and controlling purposeful behaviours.

Dr. Alan Watkins, a senior lecturer in Neuroscience and Psychological Medicine at Imperial College,

London, calls this phenomena of frontal lobe shut down a "D.I.Y. lobotomy".

The chaos causing this can happen very easily, whether you want it to or not. The heart is always beating. If you're relatively relaxed and sat in a chair the average rate will be around seventy-five beats per minute. If at any time you are put under a little bit of pressure, the heart rate starts to creep up, and anticipation or even possible anxiety will start.

The more worried you become, the more pressure you feel, the more the rate rises and the more chaos increases throughout the system. It is the natural physiological response to any challenge: increasing chaos. Many of us may still look like we are in control, but don't be deceived; the puppet master is the thing or person who is putting you under pressure, you can't control it.

Under these circumstance performance and brain function are severely compromised. There is so much tension in the system physiological chaos starts kicking in. The brain can't function when under this kind of pressure. When the signals from the heart to the brain inhibit brain function to a point of frontal lobe shut down this is called "cortical inhibition", and even the simplest of tasks becomes absolutely impossible. This happens to all of us, because the brain is built that way.

Being challenged, and it can be a challenge to your point of view, to your ego, to your relationships, in fact any type of challenge, causes this "D.I.Y. lobotomy" and you become sub-optimal immediately. And what's even more unfortunate about this state is that when the brain is inhibited it also inhibits your perception awareness so you often don't realise it's happened.

You might come out of a stressful meeting or presentation and think it went really well. But everyone else says, "What do you mean went well? It was terrible – *you* were terrible!" But because your awareness is inhibited you don't realise how bad you were. At this point we can begin to grasp the importance of honest and direct feedback! Feedback expands our awareness so that we can identify any sub-optimal behaviours, then we know what needs to change.

Cortical inhibition underpins lots of phenomena we are familiar with, things like stage fright, when you can't remember words, or at school, so many kids go blank in an exam. My absolute favourite is on *Family Fortunes*, here are a few classics from the show to illustrate the point:

- A French ferry port: "Dover."
- Something you mount: "A mountain."
- Something you lose when you get older: "Your purse."
- A type of bean: "Lesbian."
- Something you open other than a door: "Your bowels."
- A number you might have to memorise: "Seven."
- Something that makes you close your eyes: "Dark."
- A way of toasting someone: "Over a fire."
- Something that comes in pairs: "Rabbits."
- Something a policeman might say: "Spread 'em."
- A way to prevent snoring: "Put a pillow over his face."

And my own particular favourite, being from Merseyside, something associated with Liverpool: "The Yellow Brick Road."

So when your frontal lobes are inhibited, you say anything and it makes for great TV. But if you're having a meeting with your boss, with the shareholders, or maybe presenting to the board or your own department or team and you're put under pressure, you may suddenly discover that you are talking rubbish. Depending on how self-aware you are, you may hear yourself coming out with the most ridiculous nonsense, and if you do it is likely to exacerbate the situation!

As human beings we are designed and built this way; when under pressure, you get physiological chaos, instantly followed by brain shut down. All of our physiology is for survival, and believe it or not there are survival advantages to brain shut down.

Go back 200,000 years, imagine you're wandering through the forest, hunting and gathering. A huge bear comes out from behind a tree and if it sees you there then it thinks, "Ooh, lunch!". At this point you don't need any clever thinking. If you start trying to work out what kind of bear it is or which way the wind is blowing, he will catch you and eat you.

This is why you need brain shut down, your thinking has to become completely unsophisticated, to the point where it is binary. You now have two choices:

1. Fight or flight.
2. Freeze or play dead. Often this choice just happens when you drop to the ground because you've fainted.

There may be a few of you reading this who would go for the fight option and try slugging it out, but whatever you do, this binary type thinking is your only chance of survival, and anything more sophisticated will likely be the death of you.

Today, we still have the same biological mechanisms, our 200,000-year-old software has never had an upgrade! The process I'm going to describe to you will provide you with that upgrade and as long as you don't encounter any bears in the woods, it will serve you very well.

We don't meet bears today, we meet each other, and in meeting each other the same phenomena goes on. The chaos can cause somebody who is a brilliant golfer, Sergio, to lose a game after having such a great four-stroke lead, or cause a brilliant mind to give a *Family Fortunes* type answer. We can all be put off our stroke very easily, it just takes a bit of pressure.

Until you've got control of your physiology, anybody can make you look like an idiot. What's worse is you're doing it to yourself a lot of the time. Your own anxiety about your performance is actually causing the chaos, so you're lobotomising yourself! Because we have such high expectations of ourselves we are putting ourselves under pressure! There may be a lot of people around you that can trigger you into it but most of the time it's you.

So now we know why you might be brilliant one day and terrible the next; you just don't know what's going to show up that day and put you under pressure, so what can we do about it?

Until you can control your physiology – the cleverness of your thinking, your ability to come up with a great idea, innovate that sales process, or any of that stuff – the quality of your thoughts, the very things that you think and how well you think them will also be out of your control.

If we learn to control our physiology we will switch from a chaotic signal to what's called "coherence", and this produces a smooth and regular signal in the HRV.

Think About Your Thinking?

We do lots of thinking but we don't think about thinking! We just think but we don't realise that what we think and how well we think is actually influenced by something else. Thought is an emergent property from within your system. You will think different things if you're happy than if you're depressed, and how well you think the thoughts will depend on the biology.

If you what to change thinking, to double or treble the quality of your thinking, you can't do it by thinking about it! If you find a problem – caused by not thinking smart enough, you can't go home for the weekend, think about your thinking and come back thinking twenty-five per cent smarter on Monday!

Einstein said "You can't solve a problem with the same level of thinking that created the problem."

You need a new level of thinking. To get this new level you have to change the context in which thought emerges. The context in human terms is the biology – the biological context from which thought emerges is the emotional state.

195

If you change biological and emotional context then you can change the quality of the thought and the actual thought itself.

Now the good news: you don't need to be a yogic master in order to change your physiology and regain control of brain function.

It's simple - you need to influence the pattern of your breathing, which in turn affects your HRV, which affects the coherence of signals in your prefrontal cortex. The thing that absolutely underpins brain function is the ability to generate a coherent signal when reading HRV. There will still be variance, but it is stable variance as opposed to wildly fluctuating variance. That stability or coherence is the source of your brilliance.

Coherent HRV

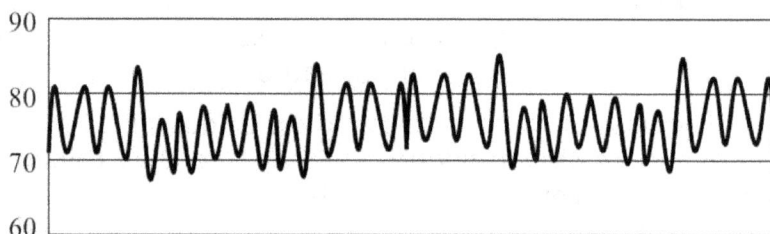

This coherent pattern is achieved with yogic breathing and leads to improved mental performance, more creativity and problem-solving, better decision-making, more flexibility in the way we think, improved memory and improved immunity to disease.

How to Achieve Coherence

Because we can get conscious control over our breathing, which controls the types of signal sent to the brain from the heart, we can use the breath to achieve physiological control by reducing and stabilising the chaos.

There are twelve different aspects of your breath that you can regulate and control. We will look at the three that are more helpful to brain function as they are key to achieving coherence:

1. Rhythm of breath pattern
2. Smoothness of breath flow
3. Attention location

The single most important aspect of the breath when creating a coherent signal from the heart to the brain is rhythm.

Rhythmic breathing will immediately change the physiology and the frontal lobe will work better. You're more perceptive, insightful, your thinking is clearer and sharper, problem solving is like second nature, and intuitively when things go wrong you can figure out what to do.

So the next time you need to calm down and someone tells you to "Take a few deep breaths", don't bother. The depth of the breath will not alter your brain function that much; it will have some affect but if we rank the aspects of breath that impact your physiology and help you calm down then depth (or volume) is at about number six.

Rhythmic breaths will immediately start to change your physiology. Try putting this to the test next time you are about to step out of your comfort zone, or if you notice you're getting worked up about something. Take a few rhythmic breaths, using a rhythm that has a fixed ratio of inhale length:exhale length. It doesn't matter what the ratio, but it has to be fixed.

Try in:out at 4:6 seconds, four seconds in and six seconds out, or you can do 3:4, 5:5 or even 6:6 – as long as it's a fixed ratio. As soon as you've established and relaxed into a rhythmic breathing pattern, the calming will begin.

The second most important thing is smoothness: even, smooth flow and pressure from start to end of both the inhale and the exhale. This will give a fixed volume per second around the entire cycle of the breath.

This aspect was described beautifully by Niranjan Gogia, one of my favourite teachers from the Yoga Institute in Mumbai. He said to imagine getting into a lift on the ground floor, the doors close smoothly and silently. You are unaware of any motion, you are simply standing still in the lift for a few moments. Then the doors slide open gracefully and there you are at the eighth floor! Now this smooth graceful operation of the lift is how you must operate your own breath, without any jerking, without any obvious change of pace, flow or direction, so smooth and graceful only you are aware of its motion.

The third aspect to consider is the location of your attention while you're breathing. Again, as with the ratio of the rhythm, this must be fixed. It is the fact that it is fixed that is most important, where it remains fixed is of lesser importance, as long as the location of the attention is focused on some aspect of your internal environment.

The Powerhouse of the Heart

Let's use the heart. Not only is the heart in the general area of the breath, in the centre of the chest, it also generates more electrical power than any other part of your system. Even thought there are billions of nerve cells up in the brain and only a couple of hundred thousand in your heart, the actual power output for your heart is about 3.5 watts, much greater than the power output from your brain, which has electrical charges that go in all different directions, scattered and often cancelling each other out. In your heart you have auto coherence, whilst the heart has to synchronise its power in order to pump.

The heart generates fifty times more electrical output than the brain, and electromagnetically it generates five thousand times more energy than the brain.

I first began to understand the power of the heart when I encountered the Institute of HeartMath – an American organisation that is all about lowering stress and building resilience. Its scientific research is extensive and has certainly helped me to appreciate my heart and how amazing and powerful it is.

I hope that you, like me, have come to the same question: "What is in control here – the head or the heart?" We have all been taught to be brain focused or brain centric in our understanding of human biology, but with all the new findings about the heart and its power I now openly question that.

Putting your attention in the heart is putting it where the primary source of power is. As if that was not enough there are other reasons to focus your attention on your heart when practicing this breathing exercise to establish coherence: dropping your attention down from your head and to your heart gets you out of your head, out of the noise, the jumble of thoughts and into the relative peace and quiet of the body. This is far less distracting and you are likely to be able to sustain the practice for longer without interruption.

And finally, "Why the heart?" Because this is where we feel love and passion, where we feel our positive emotions. So going from controlling the physiology up to the emotional state we want to generate a very positive emotional state. And many of our positive emotions are experienced in the centre of our chest. "I love you with all of my heart" – all of my head or all my brain! The awareness might be in the mind but where we feel the sensation is in the centre of the chest.

Putting your attention in the heart area will begin to put you into a more positive state, to attune you to your positive emotions.

Breathing Practice to Achieve Coherence

Fixed ratio breathing:

1. Breath in long, smooth and slow for four seconds

2. Breath out long, smooth and slow for six seconds

For consistent brilliant performance every day, follow Dr Alan Watkins' clever acronym:

B – Breathe

R – Rhythmically

E – Evenly

A – And

T – Through the

H – Heart

E – Every day

Glossary

The terms in this glossary are Sanskrit words; each word has a richness, and a depth of meaning that cannot be expressed in the brief definitions given here. If you understand that these very basic definitions are simply a guide and not definitive meanings of the words, this will assist in your comprehension of them as you find them used throughout this book

Abhinivesha	Clinging to life, fear of death, attachment to life
Achara	Routine, custom, daily practices
Adhyathma	Contemplating life with a holistic outlook
Agamah	Authority, evidence, testimony
Ahara	Inputs, procure, bring near
Ahimsa	Non-harming, non-violent.
Aishwariya	Fulfilled, confidence, self-esteem.
Ajnana	Non-knowledge, ignorance
Ananda	Bliss, ecstasy, joy
Anandamaya	Composed of bliss
Annamaya	Composed of food.
Anumana	To infer, reason, deduce
Anusharsanam	Expound, complete instruction
Aparigraha	Non-greed, accept only what is appropriate and no more.
Artha	Meaning, purpose

Asana	Posture, how you sit (within yourself)
Asmita	Sense of I, of ego that gives meaning to me and mine.
Astanga	Eight limbs, eight parts
Asteya	Honesty, not stealing or desiring what belongs to others.
Atma	The Self, the essence of life.
Avidya	Ignorance, not knowing the truth
Bhakti	Devotion
Bhava	Attitude
Buddhi	Higher intelligence
Chakra	Wheel, energy centre
Citta	Personality complex, mind
Dharana	Concentration, complete attention
Dharma	Duty, natural law
Dhyana	Meditation
Dukham	Pain, affliction, suffering
Dvesha	Repulsion, hatred
Ekagra	One pointed, focused
Guna	Quality of nature
Gunavritti	Naturally changing states of mind and matter
Hatha	Sun and moon
Jnana	Knowledge, learning, cognition

Karma	Action (cause and effect)
Karuna	Compassion
Klesha	Pain, anguish, suffering
Kosha	Sheath, layer, dimension
Kriya	Activity, (Preparatory) action
Ksipta	Disturbed state of mind
Maitri	Friendliness
Manas	Rational, instinctive mind
Manomaya	Mental, composed of mind
Mudita	Joy, gladness
Mudha	Dull, listless
Mula	Root
Nadi	Conduit, channel
Nidra	Sleep, dreams
Nirodaha	Stopping, controlling
Niruddha	Controlled
Niyama	Observance, values, ethics
Pancha	Five
Parikarma	Mental embellishment
Parimana	Change
Pramana	Right knowledge
Prana	Vital energy
Pranamaya	Composed of energy
Pranayama	Breathing practices that effect the

	vital energy
Pratyahara	Withdrawal of the senses
Raga	Attraction, attachment
Rajas	Active state of nature
Rishi	Seer, wise one,
Samadhi	Transcendental consciousness
Samskara	Habit, unconscious memory, tendency
Sattva	Harmony, balance, equanimity
Satya	Absolute truth, reality
Shraddha	Faith
Smriti	Memory
Swadyaya	Self study
Tamas	Material, dark, inert
Tapa	Diligent practice, burning desire
Upsksha	Benevolent indifference to behaviour
Vairagya	Objectivity, non-attachment
Vichara	Positive thinking
Vihara	Recreation
Vijnanamaya	Composed of higher intellect, discrimination and wisdom
Vikalpa	Imagination
Viksipta	Distracted state of mind
Viparyaya	Wrong knowledge

Vivekah	Discrimination
Vritti	Whirlwind, mental object, thought
Vyavahar	Maintaining healthy interpersonal relationships
Vyayam	Regular exercise
Yama	Values, morals, ethics
Yogachara	Yogic lifestyle

Visit the website for a downloadable and printable version of the glossary, you may find it easier to have this with you to help when reading the book.

Click to Register HERE for Exclusive Updates!

http://www.corporateyogalondon.com

EPILOGUE

Your Dying Wish

A good friend from India sent me this extract in an email. I have no idea who originally wrote it and want to give credit and thanks for the following amazing insights so.... Gratitude to the nurse in India who wrote this piece on our Dying Wishes:

For many years I worked in palliative care. My patients were those who had gone home to die. Some incredibly special times were shared. I was with them for the last three to twelve weeks of their lives. People grow a lot when they are faced with their own mortality.

I learnt never to underestimate someone's capacity for growth. Some changes were phenomenal. Each experienced a variety of emotions, as expected, denial, fear, anger, remorse, more denial and eventually acceptance. Every single patient found their peace before they departed though, every one of them.

When questioned about any regrets they had or anything they would do differently, common themes surfaced again and again. Here are the most common five:

I wish I'd had the courage to live a life true to myself, not the life others expected of me.

This was the most common regret of all. When people realise that their life is almost over and look back clearly on it, it is easy to see how many dreams have gone unfulfilled. Most people had not honoured even a half of their dreams and had to die knowing that it was due to choices they had made, or not made.

It is very important to try and honour at least some of your dreams along the way. From the moment that you lose your health, it is too late. Health brings a freedom very few realise, until they no longer have it.

I wish I didn't work so hard.

This came from every male patient that I nursed. They missed their children's youth and their partner's companionship. Women also spoke of this regret. But as most were from an older generation, many of the female patients had not been breadwinners. All of the men I nursed deeply regretted spending so much of their lives on the treadmill of a work existence.

By simplifying your lifestyle and making conscious choices along the way, it is possible to not need the income that you think you do. And by creating more space in your life, you become happier and more open to new opportunities, ones more suited to your new lifestyle.

I wish I'd had the courage to express my feelings.

Many people suppressed their feelings in order to keep peace with others. As a result, they settled for a mediocre existence and never became who they were truly capable of becoming. Many developed illnesses relating to the bitterness and resentment they carried as a result.

We cannot control the reactions of others. However, although people may initially react when you change the way you are by speaking honestly, in the end it raises the relationship to a whole new and healthier level. Either that or it releases the unhealthy relationship from your life. Either way, you win.

I wish I had stayed in touch with my friends.

Often they would not truly realise the full benefits of old friends until their dying weeks and it was not always possible to track them down. Many had become so caught up in their own lives that they had let golden friendships slip by over the years. There were many deep regrets about not giving friendships the time and effort that they deserved. Everyone misses their friends when they are dying.

It is common for anyone in a busy lifestyle to let friendships slip. But when you are faced with your approaching death, the physical details of life fall away. People do want to get their financial affairs in order if possible. But it is not money or status that holds the true importance for them. They want to get things in order more for the benefit of those they love. Usually though, they are too ill and weary to ever manage this task. It is all comes down to love and relationships in the end. That is all that remains in the final weeks, love and relationships.

I wish that I had let myself be happier.

This is a surprisingly common one. Many did not realise until the end that happiness is a choice. They had stayed stuck in old patterns and habits. The so-called "comfort" of familiarity overflowed into their emotions, as well as their physical lives. Fear of change had them pretending to others, and to their selves, that they were content, when deep within, they longed to laugh properly and have silliness in their life again. When you are on your deathbed, what others think of you is a long way from your mind. How wonderful to be able to let go and smile again, long before you are dying.

Life is a choice. It is YOUR life. Choose consciously, choose wisely, choose honestly. Choose happiness.

Maximize Your Potential

Register For Updates

I do hope you have enjoyed this, my first published book. In the hope that you'll found it really useful, there's one thing that I highly recommend you do while you go through it. Go to this special webpage designed just for you the reader, register online for free updates, worksheets and activity sheets to add real value and find your other BONUS gifts to help you on your journey. Access code "Pancha Kosha"

Do you want to:

• Raise your Employee Job Satisfaction by 20%

• Improve your Employee Retention

• Sustain your Cultural Change

Complementary charts and worksheets are available to complete online or download to guide you through the book and keep you on track.

Calculate the cost of sickness and ill health in your organisation with our free guide to the ROI.

A free quiz to identify your dosha and design your own personalised yoga routine.

"Yoga at your desk"

Get your 15min personal routine to do right now.

10% off training, coaching, classes & workshops.

Click to Register HERE for Exclusive Updates!
www.corporateyogalondon.com

www.ingramcontent.com/pod-product-compliance
Lightning Source LLC
Chambersburg PA
CBHW070534200326
41519CB00013B/3038